100 IDEAS
FOR SUPPORTING LEARNERS WITH EAL

CONTINUUM ONE HUNDREDS SERIES

100 IDEAS
FOR SUPPORTING
LEARNERS WITH
EAL

Chris Pim

Continuum One Hundreds

B L O O M S B U R Y

LONDON • NEW DELHI • NEW YORK • SYDNEY

First published 2012 by Continuum International Publishing Group

Reprinted 2012, 2013 and 2014 by Bloomsbury Education
an imprint of Bloomsbury Publishing Plc
50 Bedford Square, London W1B 3DP

Bloomsbury is a registered trademark of Bloomsbury Publshing Plc

www.bloomsbury.com

ISBN 9781441193568

@Chris Pim 2012

Printed and bound by CPI Group (UK) Ltd, Croydon CR0 4YY'

MIX
Paper from
responsible sources
FSC® C013604

CONTENTS

SECTION 1 Induction and Transition

SECTION 2 Assessment

SECTION 3 **Curriculum Access**

SECTION 6 Developing Reading

SECTION 7 Supporting Writing

My deepest thanks to Sarah Coles for her diligence in proofreading the manuscript and for her insightful suggestions for new ideas and advice on how to improve the organization of the content.

I also wish to thank these other professionals: Babette Brown (Persona Dolls), Clare Reed (Talking Partners), Julie Spencer (Talking Maths), Clare Williams (drama), Ariel Katz (sandtray technique), David Warr (Language Garden).

Acknowledgements

AfL	Assessment for Learning
BME	Black and Minority Ethnic
CoCo	Community Cohesion
CPD	Continuing Professional Development
DARTs	Directed Activities Related to Texts
EAL	English as an Additional Language
EMA	Ethnic Minority Achievement
ESL	English as a Second Language
ESOL	English for Speakers of other Languages
G&T	Gifted and Talented
ICT	Information Communication Technology
ILP	Individual Language Plan
IRC	Information Resource Centre
IWB	Interactive Whiteboard
KWL	What I Know, What I Want to Know, What I Have Learned
KS	Key Stage
LA	Local Authority
L1	First Language
LSA	Learning Support Assistant
NALDIC	National Association for Language Development in the Curriculum
NEN	National Education Network
Ofsted	Office for Standards in Education
PSHE	Personal Social Health Education
RE	Religious Education
Refed	Refugee Education
SEN	Special Educational Needs
TA	Teaching Assistant
VC	Videoconference
VLE	Virtual Learning Environment
WBRI	White British

Schools often need reassurance when dealing with learners of English as an additional language (EAL); new-arrival learners tend to cause the most concern. Yet experience shows that most learners settle quickly and make rapid progress when practitioners develop inclusive approaches to teaching and learning.

Paradoxically, research has shown that those we need to worry more about are advanced EAL learners, those who have been in the system from birth or for many years. These learners might appear to be coping well but could actually be underachieving in relation to their cognitive and academic potential.

It can be useful to group EAL learners into three distinct categories based upon their English-language proficiency. I refer to these three groups throughout the book:

- **New-to-English learners** – usually new arrivals to the United Kingdom, they are at the earliest stages of learning English.
- **Beginner EAL learners** – learners who either have acquired some English in their country of origin or have been studying for one or two years in the United Kingdom. They are likely to exhibit reasonable oral ability and may have just started to read and write independently.
- **Advanced EAL learners** – those who either have had extensive English teaching abroad, perhaps in English medium schools, or have been studying English for several years in the United Kingdom. These learners will have well-developed oral skills, will be reading and writing competently and will be approaching (or even exceeding) the attainment level of their monolingual peers across the curriculum. However, without specific intervention, many advanced learners reach a plateau in their

learning and fail to meet their full academic
potential.

Where I refer to a child's first or native language, this has
been abbreviated to L1.

Practitioners sometimes ask where they can buy or
download 'the EAL curriculum', in the mistaken belief
that there is such a resource. No such curriculum exists,
however, because EAL learners have such diverse needs.
Some EAL learners come from very academic
backgrounds; they speak and write a number of
different languages and regularly outperform their
peers. At the other extreme, some EAL learners have
had a traumatic past, with little or no prior education,
and have limited literacy even in their first language.
They may also have other needs that require specific
intervention.

In the United Kingdom, the accepted position
regarding EAL teaching and learning is that learners
best acquire English within the context of the
curriculum. Therefore, effective practice often results
from good-quality teaching and learning overall, while at
other times specific techniques and resources are needed
to meet the distinctive needs of each and every learner.
This book aims to bridge the gap between good-quality
teaching and those extra ideas that make all the
difference.

USING THE BOOK
This book is essential reading for all practitioners
working directly with EAL learners, as well as for the key
managers responsible for overseeing ethnic minority
achievement (EMA) in their school. The 100 ideas
contained within these pages aim to be both practical and
simple to implement; they use free or low-cost resources
where appropriate.

The ideas are separated into sections, such as
'Induction and Transition' and 'Encouraging Speaking

and Listening', but many of the suggested strategies and resources cross boundaries. Most of the ideas are replicable across the phases, but where a particular strategy or resource relates specifically to one group of learners, this is clearly stated.

Induction and Transition

Many schools produce general information booklets and induction materials for new-arrival families, whatever their background or L1. If this information is available at your school, adapt these materials further to reflect the major ethnic groups within the local community and to help cater for the needs of families that have recently arrived from abroad.

Where possible, try to translate the most important elements of the information available, although this may only be viable for the larger minority groups within the school. Bear in mind that some parents or carers are not fully literate in their L1 and so will not be able to access written translations. It might be a good idea to release school information through bilingual podcasts and videos hosted on the school's website.

Families who are new to the United Kingdom may have very little understanding of school processes in this country, and while we should be cautious about making generalizations, it can be useful to clearly state the school's position on various typically occurring issues.

- Explain that all learners have to study the full national curriculum (except for sex education and corporate worship).
- Offer clear guidance on homework for each year group (since some families expect more than the recommended amount).
- Identify the best and worst times to go on holiday or take extended family visits to the home country.
- Help parents to have appropriate and equitable career aspirations for all their children.
- Extend a clear invitation for families to be fully involved in all aspects of school life (in some countries it is not traditional to have significant school contact).
- Provide clear explanations of what it means to have Special Educational Needs, as some parents or carers find this 'diagnosis' hard to accept for their child.
- Explain the importance of accurately recording their child's ethnicity on the admissions form.

Where possible, meeting with the parents or carers of a newly arrived EAL learner in order to obtain important background information can be extremely beneficial.

Here are some tips to help you to prepare for a parent conference:

- Invite all parents or carers and the target learner to the meeting; let them know the focus of the meeting and its intended length in advance.
- Letters should be followed-up with phone calls; use the child's L1 where possible.
- When an interpreter is necessary, arrange for one to be present during the meeting.
- Brief interpreters before the meeting, and provide them with copies of paperwork such as school induction forms and questionnaires.
- Be flexible about timing, as both parents may work. Note that in some Muslim families a male adult may need to accompany the mother or female carer.
- Some families will have child-care requirements, as they may not have access to grandparents or a typical family-support network.

At the meeting,

- be aware that greeting customs can vary across cultures, and some adults may choose not to shake hands upon first meeting;
- seating should be arranged informally;
- when an interpreter is involved, always direct questions to the family members, maintain eye contact and gesture liberally to reinforce meaning;
- work through a set of prepared questions, and make notes as the meeting progresses; it can help to explain that the information will be confidential to the school, except where there is a required child-protection disclosure;

Set Up a Parent Conference

- ensure there is ample opportunity for the parents or carers to ask any immediate questions about the school.

At the end of the meeting, establish a review date with parents or carers to provide feedback as to how their child has settled in at the school.

As previously mentioned, it is important to gather background information about newly arrived learners as soon as possible after they start school. Try and capture details about previous schooling; for example, what subjects have or have not been studied. Find out about general aptitude, proficiency in L1 and pertinent medical, social and cultural issues. Other useful evidence includes achievement in public examinations and samples of work from country of origin. All this information will help you to develop an effective induction programme and to consider the most appropriate teaching and learning provision, including setting arrangements and other critical decisions.

You will be able to obtain much of this information at a parent conference (see Idea 2 on p.7) although sometimes this is not possible because children arrive as unaccompanied minors. At other times, lengthy communication is not possible because parents or carers have limited English and securing the services of an interpreter is not possible.

Some schools use an online background information collation tool to support this process. Such a tool presents a series of typical questions through an online form, supported through L1 audio files. While responses are mainly made through tick boxes and writing is kept to a minimum, it is recommended that a TA/LSA facilitates the use of the tool. Once complete, the system produces a written report in English that can be printed or saved and incorporated into a wider early profile.

USEFUL RESOURCE

There is a handy online background collation tool at
http://newarrivals.segfl.org.uk.

Gathering Background Information

Find Out about Languages

Finding out about the languages used within the school community really helps schools develop the most effective provision for EAL learners and their families; this is important for new arrivals as well as EAL learners who were born in the United Kingdom.

Good practice suggests that schools should gather information about the breadth of languages used by learners and their parents or carers, and should enter the information onto their assessment systems.

Here are some points for consideration.

- When new-arrival EAL learners and their families first encounter the school education system, they will feel more welcome if they get the sense that their background has been taken into consideration. When an interpreter is required, having one present at a parent conference (Idea 2 on p. 7) will help you gather critical background information.
- Class-based practitioners should prepare their classroom and their class for a new arrival by learning a few words in their L1, preparing relevant displays and gathering useful resources, including dual-language dictionaries.
- Finding out about the features of specific languages helps with L1 assessments (Idea 15 on p. 25), as well as in understanding how speaking and writing another language can impact upon how an EAL learner begins to speak and write in English. Features to consider include the written script, writing directionality, punctuation, word order and numeric symbols, among others. Find out more at www.school-portal.co.uk/ GroupWorkspaces.asp?GroupId=922202&WorkspaceI d=1567983.
- Learning about other languages gives practitioners confidence to capitalize on the linguistic knowledge and skills of their learners as inspiration for embedding intercultural work within the curriculum (Section 8); for example, language tasters, number systems and numerical methods from around the world.

- Many learners will continue to learn their L1 at home, at community language schools or both. EAL learners will appreciate schools that routinely celebrate their achievements in L1, and schools will need to consider when certain individuals are ready to be entered for oral and/or written external examinations in these languages (potentially before years 10 and 11).

Visual Timetables

School structures and routines can require a huge adjustment for younger EAL learners when they first start school, as well as for those newly arrived from abroad. Some new-arrival learners are unused to rigid timetables, while other may find it hard to understand the notion of free choice in learning. Visual timetables are a simple, practical way of tangibly presenting the abstract idea of time; they also help to reinforce the organization of events on a daily basis.

As a talking point, try displaying a large visual timetable containing movable pictures of activities at the front of the class each morning. As activities change throughout the day, pictures can be moved around; doing so helps EAL learners know which activities are in progress and what will be coming later.

Individual versions can also be useful. When there is a free choice, such as deciding on activities for 'golden-time', learners can self-determine which activities they want to tackle and in which order. It can also act as a focus of discussion between children and their parents or carers about what the child has done at school that day.

Build up a range of 'survival language' materials to support learners who are new to English. This will help them settle more easily and will enhance their interaction with adults and peers. Survival language introduces learners to essential vocabulary and simple phrases – for example, greetings, numbers, colours, time-based nouns, everyday objects and imperatives. Common questions are also useful: *'May I go to the toilet?'*

Basic language is best supported with suitable images to help convey meaning. Vocabulary fans, booklets and wall displays are all good vehicles for packaging up survival language for EAL learners. Learners who are literate in L1 will benefit from having dual-language versions, so they can transfer knowledge between languages. These learners should also be encouraged to keep a record of new language as it is encountered.

Remember, survival language is not something that needs to be specifically taught, especially if it takes time out of the curriculum. It is intended to support learners both in and out of the classroom during their first few weeks at a new school and can be given out in a pack when they arrive. It is also important not to demean learners with inappropriate materials; older learners will appreciate materials which are relatively sophisticated and supported by imagery with a more adult feel.

USEFUL RESOURCE
Survival Language (with translations) http://
    ealedinburgh.org.uk/cms/surlang.php.

Develop a Peer Buddy Programme

It is a good idea to allocate a 'peer buddy' to any new-arrival EAL learner when he or she first starts school. In fact, having a pool of potential buddies who can take turns to be with the new arrival on a daily basis will help ensure that no individual is overburdened. Potential buddies should be self-assured, trusted to model good behaviour and, most importantly, be confident speakers of English. Peers who have a shared language with the new learner can act as interpreters or translators, which is particularly important for learners who are new to English.

All buddies should undergo basic training to help them understand the requirements of the role. Buddies can support EAL learners both in and out of lessons in a number of important ways. They can help explain school routines and act as advocates for the new learner, ensuring they remain safe throughout the day. They can also support the new learner in lessons by clarifying tasks and modelling good use of English across the curriculum.

Developing a well-thought-out programme will benefit everyone. New arrivals will feel supported, and peer buddies will learn from training and from the opportunity to take on a variety of responsibilities. When the support finishes, buddies can be awarded a certificate in recognition of their efforts.

Provide new-arrival learners with a good-quality workbook and encourage them to personalize it. Workbooks can be completely blank or may contain useful resources provided by the school. For new to English learners, try developing a visual timetable (Idea 5 on p. 12), and some survival vocabulary (Idea 6 on p. 13). Include academic keywords from different subjects, maps of the world, the United Kingdom or both and a basic history timeline. A set of thumbs-up/horizontal/down flashcards or red/amber/green traffic-light cards can be useful visual tools for learners to show their level of understanding during class work.

Workbooks can be used in many different ways depending on a learner's background and level of literacy in English. All learners will benefit from using it as a notebook in which to record new vocabulary and writing in L1 and English. It can also serve as a homework communication tool whereby messages in L1 and English can be sent between home and school.

More advanced learners can use the workbook as a 'dialogue' journal to enter into a pictorial or written conversation with the class teacher or other designated key worker. Less literate learners might start with drawings and simple annotations, and more confident writers might produce extensive prose. Learners should use their dialogue journal to communicate things that are important to them; so encourage learners to write about things unrelated to the curriculum. Since meaning is more important than correct form and spelling, it helps if the dialogue partner avoids correcting anything and responds in a similar informal, chatty style. Occasionally, adult respondents may like to initiate new conversation with a key question, but in the main their contribution will involve making observational comments about what the learner has written, with the occasional follow-up question to keep the conversation moving.

Sometimes EAL learners are disorientated when they first come to live in the United Kingdom. They may find adjusting to another culture and a new home and settling in at school confusing and isolating. They may be unaware of where the United Kingdom is in relation to their home country, where their locality lies within the United Kingdom and even where their present home is in relation to the school.

This activity works well in a one-on-one situation. Start off by asking where the learner used to live; for example, 'Bangladesh'. Allow Google Earth™ to show the revolving world as it beams down to and then within a country. Work with the learner to use keywords to refine the area – for example, 'Sylhet' – or use the zoom, pan and tilt tools to find a locality that he or she can recognize. The learner may be able to identify mountain ranges, rivers, cities and other major features. Click on photographs as they appear; this may throw up images of places or scenes that the learner recognizes. All of this will generate opportunities for conversation in a natural context.

Next allow Google Earth™ to return to the United Kingdom, perhaps through other countries that the learner has lived in. Learners who have had complicated journeys may be able to trace their route from home to the United Kingdom and so provide further opportunities for discussion.

From a distance above the United Kingdom, zoom down to the area of the learner's home, along the way pointing out major features and places; it can be very motivating to zoom right down on top of the house the learner currently lives in by using the postcode. Where appropriate, places of interest can be layered onto the map to show important places within the local area.

USEFUL RESOURCE
Google Earth – www.google.co.uk/intl/en_uk/earth/index.
  html

Google Maps™ (as well as Google Earth™) is a fantastic tool for showing geographical locality, the relationship between places, distances, directions and points of interest.

Type in the postcode of a locality such as the learner's home or your school. Next, zoom out a little to show the learner's home in relation to the school. Use the 'get directions' tool to plot a route from home to school and talk. . . through the directions. Compare the route for a car journey to one on foot. Now ask the learner to describe the actual journey to school in the morning using the visual support of roads and other features along the route. Another way of doing this is to use Google Streetview™, which allows a route to be traced by clicking through real photographs of an area. Conversation produced during this type of activity is perfect for developing geographical vocabulary, locative prepositions, time-based connectives and so on.

Type keywords into the search bar to identify points of interest; for example, 'college', 'leisure centre', 'park', 'cinema'. Local places that match the keyword will be displayed on the map, ready for further investigation.

Use of Google's maps also supports the development of map skills. Switching from 'map view' to 'satellite view' and back again graphically shows how maps diagrammatically relate to actual geographical features. The distance-measurement tool can be used to show how far apart places are and to reinforce map scales.

USEFUL RESOURCE
Google Maps – http://maps.google.co.uk/

Using Google Maps™ to Teach about Locality

'Up My Street' is a website that helps residents find out more about their local area. It is particularly useful because it can help identify what services are on offer within the locality. This may be relevant not only to your target EAL learners but also to their older siblings and their parents or carers who may need to find out all sorts of legal, educational and work-related information.

As with any website, there is a level of language that needs to be mastered here; therefore, use of this website may better suit older, more advanced EAL learners and parents or carers with appropriate reading proficiency. Don't forget that it is possible to install screen readers (Idea 68 on p. 99), and run the text through translation engines (Idea 28 on p. 43), to widen access to the information. When you log on to the site, it may already 'know' and display your location, but it is easy to select any other location you choose. The most useful areas on the site are likely to be 'My neighbourhood', 'Find my nearest' and What's on'.

Find a suitable time during the school day for a practitioner to work through the website with a newly arrived learner. It is also a great opportunity to run a family-learning session for a learner with parent or carer. You may want to ask them to come prepared with their own questions; it can also be useful to prepare your own tick list of topics that need to be covered – for example, where to find local colleges, how to access ESOL classes and where to find the local leisure and emergency services.

USEFUL RESOURCE
Up My Street – www.upmystreet.com/

New-to-English software programs aim to accelerate a learner's acquisition of social and conversational skills alongside more academic aspects of language. Experience shows that these programs are most suitable for use in out-of-hours clubs and home-based learning, as well as for the occasional short-burst, time-limited intervention session. In general, they should **never** supplant good-quality mainstream teaching.

Ensure that beginner EAL learners are not isolated in front of a computer, as they need to be able to talk about the activities and the new language they are learning. For intervention sessions (Idea 21 on p. 35), ensure there is a clear language and learning focus, supported by a practitioner who is familiar with the materials. Appropriate activities might include pre-teaching vocabulary and skills for an upcoming lesson, reinforcing learning from a recent lesson and preparing for a piece of homework.

Provide EAL learners with a notebook and get them to record newly acquired language under different topics or themes or subjects. Learners who are literate in L1 need to be encouraged to translate newly acquired words and phrases into the language most familiar to them.

USEFUL RESOURCES

Education City: 'Learn English' – www.educationcity.com/uk/teachers/learn-english

2Simple :'2Start English' – www.2simple.com/2startenglish/

Cricksoft: 'New to English' – www.cricksoft.com/uk/products/content/nte

Using Sandtray to Develop Self-Expression

Children who move to England from abroad may be particularly vulnerable, and this can be compounded if they speak limited English. Some learners have also experienced significant traumas that may take a long time to unravel. What is called the sandtray technique has been successfully used with a wide range of EAL learners – regardless of language proficiency, cognitive ability or age – to facilitate non-verbal communication and storytelling by constructing a world of miniature objects within the bounds of a sandtray. Sandtray therapy is a therapeutic intervention that requires training before using the medium. If you are not trained, you can support children's self expression by referring them to someone trained in sandtray techniques.

This kinaesthetic experience can help children to manage difficult emotions, organize themselves mentally to augment learning, feel a sense of control and mastery, connect with others, work through personal struggles and conflicts in the safety of metaphor, rehearse challenging situations and find their voice, regardless of their language skills.

In sandtray technique, children are encouraged to sculpt sand into a landscape where the blue sides of the tray form the skyline and water can be represented wherever the blue surface of the tray shows through the sand. With learners working individually or as part of a group, miniature objects are selected to play out a scenario or build up a final scene, or 'exhibit'.

MATERIALS
- clean sand
- rectangular sandtrays – approximately 23 inches long by 18 inches wide by 3.5 inches deep and painted blue (to represent sea and sky) on the inside
- miniature objects such as plastic animals or people; natural objects; bridges, fences or buildings; vehicles; small religious artefacts

RUNNING DIFFERENT TYPES OF SESSIONS

Learners work individually, each with a tray and set of objects. They can be supported passively by an adult observer who acts as a witness to the event. Orally confident learners can be encouraged to explain their 'exhibit' or narrate their own 'story'. This could be done in English or L1 where appropriate. The children can also be given the opportunity to write, using their 'world' as a visual story outline.

Extra sandtrays can be made available so that learners can use more than one at a time. Often children with two contrasting world experiences like to show their worlds as separate. In this way they can explore the feelings and sensations unique to each world.

Sandtray is a creative, expressive medium and helps children communicate when using words is difficult. Strong feelings can come up when using sandtray, and so it is important that the children be allowed to express themselves creatively. Don't correct their grammar or their story when using this medium to facilitate language; it is vital to respect the learner's creation and not touch it or interfere with it. It can either be dismantled by the learner at the end or by the professional after the learner has left. Children who are proud of their creation may give permission for a photo to be taken of it. Because the work is deeply personal, their permission needs to be obtained before showing it to others.

Assessment

Bilingual helpers will ordinarily be peripatetic or school-based practitioners, but don't underestimate the role that parents and learners themselves can have in supporting interpreting and translation. It is therefore a good idea to perform an audit on the whole school community in order to identify who can speak, read and write different languages and with what level of proficiency. An informal chat involves a different level of language proficiency and maturity than a formal assessment that requires an individual to have good L1 proficiency as well as a full understanding of the need to be confidential.

It is often helpful to have an interpreter present during a parent conference [Idea 2 on p. 7], in order to gather critical background information. Let the parents or carers know that interpreters will be available for parents' evenings or review days; they will be more likely to attend as a consequence. A formal assessment of L1 [Idea 15 on p. 25], requires the services of a skilled interpreter or translator, preferably an independent individual with a solid educational background. This will help you gain an unbiased, realistic picture of the varying proficiencies that a learner has in a language other than English.

Interpreting and translation need to be an integral part of a school's support mechanism. Should it prove impossible to find appropriate help within the community and local authority, you may need to look farther afield. For example, most areas provide phone lines and interpreting/translation services for a set fee depending on requirements.

It is really useful to know about the full language repertoire of everyone within the school community. For new-arrival EAL learners, an accurate assessment of proficiency in their L1, as well as other influencing languages, will help build a more complete picture of their general ability.

Relevant information should include the following:

- the language considered to be L1, as well as all other languages used;
- how long each language has been studied and when and for what purpose is it used
- proficiency in speaking, listening, reading and writing L1.

A rigorous assessment of L1 is best achieved in collaboration with speakers of the same language, particularly adults with an academic background, as they should be able to establish if the learner is functioning at an age-appropriate level. Sometimes it is not possible to secure the services of a trained bilingual practitioner; it may be necessary to seek help from parents or even older peers, although impartiality and personal privacy should always be guaranteed in such cases.

School-based practitioners should not be dissuaded from assessing a child's L1 simply because bilingual support is unavailable at the time. Recordings of conversation, reading and samples of writing can be reviewed at a later date. Moreover, many significant details of L1 proficiency can be ascertained by any skilled practitioner

Where possible, an L1 assessment should include the following:

- watching informal conversation between peers;
- observing more formal dialogue between the learner and a bilingual adult;

- while a learner reads from a familiar and age-appropriate text, listening for pace, intonation and self-correction;
- checking if the learner is reading for meaning;
- sampling writing about a familiar story, setting or situation; consider overall length, handwriting, demarcation, evidence of self-correction, grammar and sophistication in use of language.

It is evident that some EAL learners also have additional special educational needs. However, experience suggests that when learners are experiencing problems at school, looking to attribute difficulties to an underlying SEN is usually not the most relevant of starting points.

First, don't rely purely on standardized tests, as EAL learners do not generally demonstrate their true capability because of the potential language demand. Even non-verbal tests have inherent cultural bias that can depress scores. Ensure that learners have been well settled in the school over a period of several weeks before carrying out any formal tests.

It is important to gather a range of evidence to help inform any decisions either way. For example,

- information from parents or carers about the child's previous educational experience;
- observation of learners both in and out of class;
- assessment of L1 proficiency (Idea 15 on p. 25),
- analysis of English proficiency and progress over time (it is quite usual for EAL learners to have an uneven profile of achievement across the curriculum).

Take a diagnostic approach, and ask questions about all aspects of a learner's experience. Doing so will allow you to filter out irrelevant information and focus on factors that can't be explained by things like incomplete education, language, culture or a traumatic past. Some schools use SEN or EAL 'filter questions' to help them identify whether observable difficulties are a result of EAL or more indicative of SEN. When in doubt, seek advice from trained specialists in this area.

USEFUL RESOURCE
SEN or EAL filter questions – www.school-portal.co.uk/ GroupDownloadFile.asp?GroupId=922201&Resourc eId=2765573

Evidence from 2007 PLASC data* has shown that at national level there has been an under-representation of EAL learners on schools' G&T registers. It is useful to know whether this continues to happen locally and, more specifically, within a particular school or setting.

Good practice suggests that the representation of EAL (and BME) learners should be broadly in line with that of the white British (WBRI) population. Consider asking these questions when there is an under-representation of EAL learners:

- What might be the implications of an under-representation?
- What criteria does the school use to identify G&T learners?
- Are the criteria flexible enough to ensure fair and equitable opportunities to identify BME/EAL learners – in particular, those who are new to English?

Learners identified as G&T may be able to draw down additional support or access specific enrichment activities. Here are some ideas that may be particularly pertinent to EAL learners:

- Use EAL learners with strong L1 skills as school interpreters or translators; consider training them through a 'young interpreter' scheme (Idea 97 on p. 144).
- Encourage learners to offer L1 taster classes for their peers.
- Celebrate the L1 learning achievements of EAL learners at complementary language schools.
- When they are ready, enter learners for oral and written national examinations in their L1.
- Offer enterprise opportunities for those BME/EAL learners who actively contribute to running family businesses.

*Monaghan, F., 'Gifted and Talented statistics: PLASC data and EAL', *Naldic Quarterly,* 5(1), pp. 35–39.

USEFUL RESOURCE
Realising Equality and Achievement for Learners (REAL), London Gifted and Talented – www. realproject.org.uk/

How are learners expected to demonstrate progress and attainment within any particular curriculum area? This is an important question, because every EAL learner is at a different stage in the acquisition of English. In particular, those new to English will struggle to demonstrate the full extent of their learning through a predominately monomodal written outcome.

For beginner EAL learners, look for feedback through facial expression, mime and gesture. It can be useful to employ a traffic light system, where green demonstrates full understanding, amber indicates the user is unsure and red indicates confusion. Where possible, use bilingual interpreters to help facilitate oral feedback. Allow learners to produce annotations and writing in L1; translation can always be done at a later time.

Routine use of mini-whiteboards will encourage learners to produce regular visual feedback about their learning through ticks, smiley faces, words and short phrases. Understanding can also be conveyed by learners through pictures and completion of graphic organizers (Idea 39 on p. 54), such as tables, charts, diagrams and Mind Maps (Idea 37 on p. 52). It will also prove beneficial to enable learners to show learning through digital media such as audio recordings, photographs and short video clips.

All EAL learners should be working towards language targets, whether they are new to English, beginners or more advanced learners. It is important to ensure that targets are appropriate, achievable and challenging and are reviewed on a regular basis. It is also good practice to involve learners in the development and review of their own targets.

Appropriate targets need to match the stage of language development of the learner. Some targets may operate globally across the curriculum, while others need to be designed within a more subject-specific context. Compare the following targets: *Begin to use paragraphs* and *Begin to demarcate experimental reports using topic headings*. Subject-specific targets work best when they support a wider global target; this helps to ensure that all practitioners take responsibility for 'language teaching' rather than just leaving it to the English department or EAL key worker.

It is good practice to create individual language plans (ILPs) for EAL learners in order to establish a whole-school focus on specific aspects of speaking, listening, reading and writing across the curriculum.

USEFUL RESOURCES

New-Arrival Assessment Guidelines for Primary and Secondary Schools, Portsmouth Ethnic Minority Achievement Service – www.school-portal.co.uk/GroupWorkspaces.asp?GroupId=922201&WorkspaceId=1568035.

Assessing English as an Additional Language: Guidelines for Primary and Secondary Schools, Hillingdon Ethnic Minority Achievement Support Service – www.hillingdongrid.org/microsite/emass/index.php.

Targets and Individual Language Plans (ILPs)

Curriculum Access

How to Group EAL Learners

Making the right decisions about grouping and setting is essential to enable all EAL learners to reach their full potential. As a general rule, EAL learners need to be grouped according to their academic potential rather than their proficiency in English. A curriculum that matches the cognitive ability of the learner will build upon existing skills, help to maintain motivation and raise self-esteem.

EAL learners benefit from being surrounded by orally proficient speakers of English, who can model effective use of language across the curriculum. In class discussions, offer EAL learners the opportunity to rehearse their ideas with a supportive peer prior to answering in front of the class. In a larger group, EAL learners will appreciate hearing a two-way conversation between confident English speakers. When using computers, try not to isolate EAL learners; instead pair them with a good-language role model.

It is a good idea to pair same-language speakers together. Being able to converse and think through ideas in a familiar language can really benefit learners, particularly those new to English. As learners become more orally proficient, they will naturally begin to convert their thoughts into English, which will allow them to participate confidently in colloquial conversation and prepare them for more formal oral and written tasks.

Finally, take a flexible approach to the physical placement of learners within the room. EAL learners should have a clear view of the board and be close to the class teacher; however, they shouldn't be isolated or made to feel conspicuous.

The best place for EAL learners to do their learning is within the mainstream classroom. There are times, however, where it may be appropriate to withdraw learners from the classroom for some specific intervention – for example, when it is really clear that the whole-class activity can't be made accessible enough for the target learner.

Ensure there is a clear language focus for the work, and try to keep sessions short – no longer than 20 minutes, two or three times per week. Vary the timing of slots in order to avoid missing the same mainstream classes, and try to avoid practical lessons or subjects such as languages where EAL learners tend to perform well.

Think carefully about group composition, as it is important for EAL learners to work with peers that can model secure use of language, both orally and within literacy tasks. Thus, forming groups that only contain beginner EAL learners may not be the most appropriate arrangement. Finally, identify teachers and TAs/LSAs that have had specific EAL training; they are likely to be the most successful at withdrawal intervention sessions.

It is important that all tasks meet the cognitive and academic level of the target learners. In addition, learners will benefit from content that has a meaningful context – in other words, work that is directly linked to the curriculum or a sequence of activities that form part of an extended project.

Appropriate activities for withdrawal intervention include the following:

- orientation exercises for new arrivals (Ideas 9–11 on pp. 16–18);
- use of 'new to English' materials (Idea 12 on p. 19);
- involvement in an established intervention strategy; for example, talking partners (Idea 98 on p. 145);
- pre-teaching of key vocabulary and concepts for upcoming lessons (see idea (Idea 43 on p. 58);
- post-teaching to consolidate work from mainstream classes;

Withdrawal Intervention

- games-based activities that focus on oral development for beginner EAL learners;
- teaching to address specific gaps in literacy for advanced EAL learners;
- extended projects that integrate speaking, listening, reading and writing; making talking books or digital storytelling (Ideas 46–48 on page 64–67);

EAL learners experience the double challenge of having to learn curriculum content alongside the academic language associated with different subjects and activities. It is therefore essential that practitioners consider the specific language demands of any particular curriculum area and plan their lessons accordingly.

Observing peers in their teaching, watching pre-recorded sessions or both will enable practitioners to unravel the particular language needed for EAL learners to access key tasks as well as demonstrate full achievement. In this way specific language demands can be identified and written into curriculum plans.

The language embedded within any subject or activity inherently involves the use of specialist vocabulary and frequently used phrases as well as the more specific functions and features of both oral and written language. Some EAL learners have already mastered many of these subject-specific language conventions in their L1, while others may have significant gaps. Above all, it should be remembered that planning to tackle the language demands of the curriculum will benefit not only EAL learners but also their monolingual peers, as everyone needs to learn academic language that goes beyond everyday situations.

A useful planning frame for analysing language demands is shown below.

Curriculum Objectives	Key Activities	Language Functions	Language Features	Language Structures	Academic Vocabulary
Desired outcomes	What will be done by learners	Techniques required in use of language; e.g. comparing, explaining, predicting	Tone, style, voice, figurative language, grammar	Examples of linking words and specific phrases; e.g. conditionals, cause and effect	Context-related words

Bloom's Taxonomy

As you plan language support for your EAL learners, it can be easy to forget the importance of providing cognitively demanding tasks.

Try referencing Bloom's taxonomy on a regular basis to ensure activities challenge learners to use their higher-order thinking skills, such as creating and evaluating, alongside lower-level processes such as the simple process of remembering. With appropriate support, most EAL learners can reach every level on the framework.

At times you will want to plan relatively simple tasks that give learners an immediate sense of achievement; for example, naming objects on flashcards, labelling diagrams, sequencing story visuals and conducting dictionary races. However, you also need to design much more sophisticated activities, such as asking learners to analyse information from a range of sources and argue a case or write persuasively in favour of a particular position. As you work your way up the framework, learners will require increased support to access content, participate orally and create written outcomes. An example would be when learners are asked to evaluate a scientific method. Bear in mind that you may have to adjust expectations for beginner EAL learners, perhaps anticipating an oral contribution rather than a formal written outcome (Idea 18 on p. 30).

Bloom's taxonomy

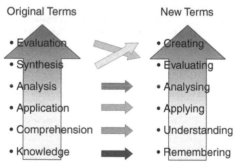

Original Terms

- Evaluation
- Synthesis
- Analysis
- Application
- Comprehension
- Knowledge

New Terms

- Creating
- Evaluating
- Analysing
- Applying
- Understanding
- Remembering

The National Strategies Secondary CPDM 4 – Talk as a Tool for Thinking

Practise Message Abundancy

Rather than simplifying tasks for EAL learners, use 'message abundancy' techniques – teaching sequences that present the key messages in a variety of ways. This offers several opportunities for learners to pick up and absorb new language and concepts.

In certain situations message abundancy happens naturally. For example, when giving oral explanations, practitioners tend to make the same point several times using mime, gesture and plenty of visual clues. During question-and-answer sessions, learners also appreciate how practitioners seamlessly recast their language, correcting mistakes naturally by replacing colloquial terminology with more academic forms. For example in a science discussion, recasting a sentence using the word 'mass' when the learner had erroneously used the word 'weight'.

EAL learners benefit from having several opportunities to access the same curriculum content. A sequence might include the following: watching a short video clip, followed by text marking of written material and finally having a paired discussion that draws out the main points.

Reading tasks can be supported by Directed Activities Related to Texts (Idea 67 on p. 98). In preparation for writing tasks, it can be useful to encourage learners to part-process information using graphic organizers (Idea 39 on p. 54). Additionally, talk-for-writing approaches enable learners to revisit more formal use of language and concepts – useful activities include oral presentations, hot-seating (Idea 55 on p. 79) and Socratic talk (Idea 63 on p. 91). Of course, modelling expected outcomes is also crucial for EAL learners.

USEFUL RESOURCE

'Message abundancy' is a term coined by Pauline Gibbons (see Gibbons, P. (2006). *Bridging discourses in the ESL classroom: Students, teachers and researchers.* London: Continuum.

Utilize L1 Skills

As already discussed (Idea 20 on p. 34); it helps to group same-language learners together so they can collaborate in a preferred language during oral and written tasks.

Encourage more advanced learners to annotate text in L1 during reading tasks. This will link academic and linguistic knowledge acquired in other situations and help with internalizing new language. Provide EAL learners with vocabulary/phrase notebooks so that they can build up personal bilingual language lists.

Learners can also use L1 in writing tasks. Allow new-to-English learners to draft writing in a more familiar language. This will enable them to order their thoughts and write more freely, making and correcting mistakes as they progress. There is sound educational thinking in this approach, as they will be able to partake in cognitively demanding work where they will be developing subject knowledge alongside their peers. At a later time you may be able to get the writing translated. Moreover, more advanced EAL learners will begin to make partial translations for themselves; for example, by writing a sentence or so in English after they have done the L1 drafting.

Use your bilingual learners as a resource within the classroom. They will be able to enrich the lives of other children in the class – for example, by conversing in other languages and writing in different scripts. They may be able to offer interesting verbal and mathematical insights, such as where words borrowed from other languages come from and how number systems and numerical methods work in other countries.

Build up a comprehensive range of bilingual dictionaries in the library or resources centre ready to be loaned to EAL learners when required. Suggest that parents purchase portable bilingual dictionaries for their children, and encourage the learners to bring them to school every day. Be aware that print-only bilingual dictionaries will only be useful when learners have well-developed literacy in L1. It is possible, however, to resource versions that provide audio support through CD-ROMs and TalkingPENs (Idea 60 on p. 87). When looking up English words, you may find that learners who are insecure in sequencing the letters of the English alphabet take an unacceptable length of time to find the right word. For this reason they may be better off with visual dictionaries that tend to organize words thematically.

Just because learners have the ability to translate between languages does not mean they know how to make the best use of a dictionary. Ensure learners don't just translate the first matching word they find in the dictionary. They should be aware that some words have synonyms and they need to consider each meaning to be sure they have the correct word before translation. They will also benefit from knowing how to use phonetic spelling to pronounce words, how to check the part of speech of a word and how to identify collocations (Idea 75 on p. 109);

During writing tasks, some learners construct texts in their head using their L1. Subsequently they will make a translation into English before committing the words to paper. Encourage learners to look up translations of appropriate words that they know in L1 – this will help learners develop a more varied English vocabulary.

USEFUL RESOURCES

Milet – www.milet.com/dictionaries.asp
Mantra Lingua – www.mantralingua.com/
Grant & Cutler – www.grantandcutler.com/

Bilingual Dictionaries

Electronic Translation Devices

Portable electronic translation devices can be really useful, particularly for older, more advanced EAL learners who are literate in L1. These tools become more sophisticated all the time, but they do have their limitations. For example, the difficulty with understanding context within a sentence can result in the software translating the wrong homograph.

Most translation devices contain comprehensive bilingual dictionaries that are most appropriate for translating keywords, short phrases and colloquial expressions. Some devices can also output oral translations in authentic synthesized voices and even register speech in a target language, providing feedback on the accuracy of pronunciation. Up-to-date translators can scan text through a pointing device ready for translation and even register speech in one language and output oral translation in another.

If you are working in a school with large numbers of learners from particular language groups, you may benefit from having one or more of these devices to loan to learners on a daily basis. Ensure the learners have the technology available during mainstream lessons to clarify everyday language as well more academic terminology. It is useful for class teachers to prepare simple, concise lesson aims that will give unambiguous, meaningful translations. Help learners focus on the weaknesses of translation by considering synonyms that cause ambiguity – for example, root (scientific and mathematical), root (grammar), roots (idiomatic).

Encourage same-language speakers to talk about translation and make comparisons between languages; this will help them notice patterns that make sense to them and allow them to think about structure and purpose in use of language. Also, suggest to learners that they practise and get feedback on pronunciation using the text-to-speech analyser.

USEFUL RESOURCE
ECTACO – www.ectaco.co.uk/

Online there are many free translation tools that can support communication and curriculum access. It's worth spending some time researching which ones are acknowledged as the most accurate and user-friendly. This could involve bilingual practitioners, parents and the learners themselves. For new-to-English learners, a translation engine can be one of the few ways to facilitate two-way communication in the absence of a bilingual practitioner.

Translation engines are generally better than hand-held devices at translating paragraphs of text because they match text to known human translations and thus render a more accurate translation. Translation engines can translate pasted text or even entire web pages, but be aware that some languages render better translations than others. For example, Romance languages tend to be reasonably accurate, whereas German is often less successful. However, never rely on machine translation for formal communication. When using the tool for a two-way dialogue, ensure that each user types simple, single clauses rather than complex sentences, as this will result in a more accurate translation. Try reversing the translation through the translation tool to check for accuracy. Note that some engines enable a user to hear the translation as well as read the rendered text – a useful addition for learners who are not so literate in L1.

Some advanced EAL learners can also benefit from installing web browser plug-ins that provide access to bilingual dictionaries without ever having to leave a web page that is being read. This will be useful for learners who are reading English well but still struggle with academic language and who will be able to transfer understanding of words and phrases from a stronger L1.

USEFUL RESOURCES
Google Translate – http://translate.google.com/
Foreign word – http://foreignword.com/
g-Translate for Firefox – https://addons.mozilla.org/
    en-us/firefox/addon/gtranslate

Online Translation Tools

Set Up Computers to Use Different Language Scripts

If your learners want to be able to use ICT for learning in L1, then it is important that the computer be set up to allow them to read their own languages in documents and on the internet. Also, they need to be able to input the full range of characters in their written script through the keyboard. This will allow them to use translation tools effectively, type their own script in word processors and use keywords to search for web pages in their own language.

Modern operating systems include full character sets of all the major scripts across the world; these are called unicode fonts. Occasionally documents or web pages display unreadable characters; this means that you will need to get one or more extra fonts installed. This is simply a matter of downloading the appropriate font and copying it into the Fonts subfolder within the main Windows folder.

Windows keyboards are really easy to set up for other languages. The specific procedure may be slightly different for each version of Windows, but the first place to look is in the control panel. Here you will find the option to be able to change the keyboard set-up to allow other language input. Once a new keyboard has been installed, it can be accessed from an icon on the taskbar (bottom right of the main window). Simply click the icon to switch back and forth between available keyboards.

Using a projector can be a good way to help EAL learners focus on the task, due to the audio-visual nature of this aid. You can use the projector to enlarge resources, deliver multimedia content and model practical or literacy-based learning. Once learners are focused towards the front, you will be able to scan their faces for understanding. Of course, when projectors are hooked up to interactive whiteboards, you can also involve learners more kinaesthetically through the touch-sensitive surface.

Visualizers can add another dimension to your teaching, allowing you to make meaning more explicit for EAL learners. They are useful for enlarging small objects for demonstration purposes (such as for dissection), for looking at small animals or plants or for examining artefacts like coins or integrated circuits. Visualizers are perfect for showing a top-down view of how to do something – for example, modelling cursive script, highlighting the procedure for using the memory button on a calculator, modelling the correct use of a protractor or demonstrating how to measure distance on a map using a piece of string. It is also possible to perform a shared reading, with the additional advantage of being able to show the visuals alongside the text.

Visualizers provide an immediate way to show the whole class a piece of work in progress; for example, group planning in the form of a storyboard or concept map, an incomplete piece of art work, a first draft of a piece of writing. This helps to model expectations for learners and encourage peer review. You can also get wireless versions of visualizers, so that you can walk around the room and project work instantly onto the whiteboard with the minimum of interruption to the class.

Data Projectors and Visualizers

Use of Images 1

Access to good-quality images, whether printed or digital, is essential for working with EAL learners. It is worth building up a good selection to support topics or subjects across the curriculum. There really is truth in the old adage that a picture is worth a thousand words; a carefully chosen image will make ideas and concepts much more explicit.

Try developing cognitively demanding tasks for new-to-English learners that are non-verbal and kinaesthetic in nature, such as those that require manipulation of printed or digital images. For example, encourage learners to:

- sort photographs based on particular criteria, such as a historical time period;
- use collage as a framework for comparing and contrasting ideas; for example, settings, characters or themes within or between familiar stories;
- match images together; for example, photographs of art from the same artist, style or artistic movement;
- rank images on set criteria, such as mathematical scale;
- develop a visual narrative from a set of images to explain a sequence of events: a physical, chemical or biological process, the causes of a historical incident or an environmental disaster;
- choose historical visual sources to support a particular point of view;
- interpret details in one image by overlaying with another, such as when matching a map to a satellite photograph;
- predict details in obscured parts of an image; for example, continue a trend in a graph or draw in the missing organisms in a food web.

Images are also excellent for developing oracy and literacy across the curriculum. Projecting images onto the whiteboard at the start of a lesson helps to contextualize work coming up later or to recap content from a previous lesson. Get learners to discuss a mystery object, find the link between a rolling set of images or spot the odd one out. Show a close-up of an image and ask the class to theorize about its identity – this is an excellent way to model the use of modal verbs. Images also help support show-and-tell activities and presentations as well as form the focus for class debates (Idea 63 on p. 91).

Get learners to talk in depth about one or more images; this encourages the use of more formal talk that helps to bridge the gap between thinking, talking and writing. Some learners have difficulty with annotating their artwork; reviewing each other's work helps reinforce technical language and model language structures that they will need to use in their writing. Talking about historical or geographical visual sources will help learners pick out relevant language for extended writing activities.

Annotating images, digitally or in print, also helps develop media literacy. Ask learners to write a caption for what is happening in a photograph or design a snappy slogan for a product. Ask them to annotate different parts of an image, for example an X-ray or ultrasound, a painting of the crucifixion, an image of war, a photograph of a disaster zone or a Heath Robinson drawing. Again, short annotations encourage the use of a more formal, academic style of writing, particularly for description and explanation. You can also stimulate creative writing by getting learners to talk and write about a series of connected book illustrations without the text.

USEFUL RESOURCE
NEN Gallery – http://gallery.nen.gov.uk/

Use of Audio

As they progress through the early stages of acquiring English, many EAL learners hear and understand better than they read and write. Where possible, provide learners with oral access to key texts in order to make meaning more explicit. Oral versions of books and poems can often be found on CDs, and digital books can be listened to on e-book readers. Set up screen-reading software (Idea 68 on p. 99) on computers so that digital texts can be orally delivered to a learner.

Find audio files or podcasts that demonstrate particular aspects of language use across the curriculum. You could play famous speeches to demonstrate use of formal, standard English. Radio plays or shows might be useful for modelling more informal talk and highlighting the differences in regional accents. A quick search on the internet can reveal a multitude of podcasts for reinforcing curricular learning. There are also podcasts that focus more on the conversational language required for different everyday contexts.

Songs can be useful for consolidating what learners already know; they lend themselves naturally to listening tasks. For example, get learners listening to songs like 'Dem Bones' or 'The Elements' and ask them to identify key scientific vocabulary. Certain songs are perfect for demonstrating particular grammatical features, and lyrics can be used for active reading, such as text marking and reconstruction exercises.

Don't forget how powerful music is for conveying meaning. For example, a suitable sample of music could be useful for reinforcing meter and mood in a particular poem.

USEFUL RESOURCES
Audio network – http://audio.e2bn.net/
ESL Pod – www.eslpod.com/

When used selectively, video can help to reinforce hard-to-explain topics within subject areas. Try showing short clips rather than extensive sections; beginner EAL learners in particular will find it hard to concentrate on this type of activity for long periods of time. Prepare one or two questions to focus attention, or provide a simple graphic organizer (Idea 39 on p. 54) in which to record key information.

EAL learners will appreciate the opportunity to watch films and TV versions of key texts; this will help reinforce the plot as well as bring characters and settings to life. Films on DVD usually offer the option to show English subtitles, which can be beneficial for some EAL learners. Indeed, it is possible to get subtitles in other languages, which may help beginner EAL learners who are literate in L1.

Occasionally, try showing video without the sound, as this puts all learners in the same position. Encourage learners to discuss what is happening in the scene, or ask them to consider what just happened or predict what is about to happen.

Useful digital video can be found on the internet; if a site is blocked, try a download from an alternative venue. YouTube can be a good source for digital material – but, as always, all videos need to be checked to ensure they include only appropriate language and content. TrueTube, a more educational site, offers videos that may prove helpful for RE, PSHE and Citizenship lessons.

USEFUL RESOURCE
TrueTube – www.truetube.co.uk/

IDEA 35

Tablet Devices

Recent technological developments have led to an explosion in mobile devices with touch-sensitive surfaces. Whether you are a peripatetic support teacher, a consultant going in and out of different schools or a school-based practitioner, these devices have huge potential for supporting EAL learners. Tablet computers come in different shapes and sizes, driven by different operating systems that support a wide-variety of applications (or apps). You will probably want to invest in devices that have one or more cameras and 3G (or better) connectivity for use when a Wi-Fi network is unavailable.

The advantages of tablet computers include portability, connectivity to the internet and other networks and the natural touch-sensitive surface that is supportive for learners unfamiliar with keyboards and mice. Encourage learners to use the audio-recording facility to capture thoughts and ideas as well as for curriculum-based work. They can use the inbuilt camera to take snapshots or short video clips, to record their achievements and to give non-verbal feedback to their class teachers. There is also the potential for participation in simple videoconferencing (Ideas 90–91 on pp. 132–133). Where appropriate, enable learners to use online translation tools, electronic dictionaries, mapping tools and so on. The e-book reading capability brings texts alive in a multi-modal way, and it is a good idea to source e-books to suit different types of learners.

While these devices have resonance for individual use, you will find greater applicability for collaborative learning, where the device and software become the focus. Quite apart from the inbuilt tools, there are free and low-cost apps (Idea 36 on p. 51) to support curriculum access and creativity. Group-based learning with tablet computers inherently supports speaking and listening through physical or online communication, as well as providing opportunity for shared reading and writing experiences.

The range of educational apps for tablet devices grows on a daily basis, and you will want to thoroughly review each one before use. Apps are generally developed for a particular market and tend to target a specific age range.

Since 'apps' are likely to have a language demand that must be overcome before they become useful for an EAL learner,

- experiment with some of the many different flashcard applications; they make it easy to produce interactive activities to support the acquisition of vocabulary;
- capitalize on e-book technology to give EAL learners access to digital texts; inbuilt tools offer users the ability to kinaesthetically interact with the pages of the book, instantly look up word meanings, highlight text and have text read aloud through text-to-speech synthesis;
- download 'apps' to support creative writing, such as digital 'story cubes', cartoon creators like 'Comic Life' or 'Our Story'; explorable 3-D worlds are also perfect for generating discussion and descriptive writing;
- install a range of mapping tools such as Google Maps™ or Earth to support induction for new arrivals.

Note that some apps, such as Google Goggles™ and QR code readers, interface with inbuilt cameras to provide access to information. There are also numerous subject-based apps to reinforce learning, as well as those that purport to teach English. These types of apps vary in quality and need careful thought before being used with target EAL learners.

USEFUL RESOURCE
iPads in Education – www.ipadineducation.co.uk/
    iPad_in_Education/Welcome.html

Mind Maps

A spider diagram is an example of a simple mind map that you might use to elicit prior knowledge at the beginning of a topic. Draw one central idea on the whiteboard, and build up a hierarchy of connected words or phrases along different branches of the diagram. Most EAL learners will appreciate time to think and talk through ideas before responding in a whole-class situation. This could also be organized as a small-group activity using marker pens and sugar paper. In order to ensure participation from all learners, give each learner a different-coloured marker, and make it the whole group's responsibility to ensure a reasonable spread of colour.

Mind maps are more likely to develop throughout a topic rather than at the start, although they can be an effective way to summarize learning at the end. In a mind map, learners need to be more organized and consistent about how they link ideas together. Ensure learners keep each branch of the map to a single colour; this has been shown to assist recall of information. Suggest that learners annotate with single words or very short phrases, using print rather than writing. Finally, encourage the use of images or symbols or icons, as these can convey ideas more simply than printed words. Encourage learners to use their mind maps as a revision aid, or perhaps display them prominently in the classroom. You may also want to keep a colour photocopy of some of the best ones to use as stimulus material for future work.

USEFUL RESOURCE
Mind-mapping software: FreeMind – http://freemind.
   sourceforge.net/wiki/index.php/Main_Page

Key visuals are information packages; they aid understanding by showing the relationships between content, concepts and language. They enable learners to move beyond basic 'naming language' into higher-order thinking, including explanation, hypothesis and prediction (Idea 23 on p. 38). In science, for example, food webs and pyramids of numbers conceptually show how organisms are connected with each other and with their environment. Here, the size and position of graphical elements, such as pictures and symbols, imply semantic relationships; together with concise text, they help learners recall both colloquial and academic language.

Introduce a topic by showing a key visual, and keep it in a visible place throughout the work. This is an excellent way to illustrate complex ideas and introduce or reinforce academic language.

Encourage learners to conduct paired or group work around 'the water cycle' or another key visual. Invite learners to piece together an incomplete version using information drawn from other sources. Incomplete versions would also work well as a barrier game (Idea 58 on p. 84) for a pair of learners.

Key visuals are self-contained narratives that support the development of explanatory writing. A historical key visual, like a diagram of the triangular slave trade, conveys factual information alongside concepts. Using this type of resource, ask learners to produce an explanation of the cycle of events. This helps to develop texts that have a logical structure, varied use of academic vocabulary, cause-and-effect language and copious use of time connectives.

Sometimes it is useful to get learners to create their own key visuals to help them remember specific information. When studying a book on, for example, a historical event, get learners to produce a story map to illustrate the main plot, settings, characters and so on. The developmental process will help reinforce the sequence of events and main facts and act as a trigger for information recall at a later date.

Graphic Organizers

EAL learners benefit from approaches that help break information and language down into manageable chunks. Graphic organizers take the form of blank templates that act as a holding area for different types of information. Use graphic organizers when learners are required to process a lot of information before a formal presentation or piece of writing.

To illustrate the use of graphic organizers, consider the following activity. A year 7 class has been asked to investigate the pros and cons of building a dam in a particular locality. They need to collate evidence from a range of sources and use the information to write a discursive text that presents all the arguments. A learner could use a simple table to sort information into two groups – pros and cons. Additionally, he or she might choose a Venn diagram to help organize information into impacts that affect humans, the environment or both. Having part-processed the information, EAL learners will find the language demands of the writing task much easier, because they can simply refer to the table or Venn diagram rather than having to reread the original source material. Staging a task like this really supports EAL learners in more formal oral and written tasks.

Here are some examples of different types of graphic organizers:

Organizational Mechanism	Type of Organizer
Sorting	retrieval charts, tree diagrams
Sequencing	storyboards, timelines, flow-charts, branching diagrams, cycles
Making logical connections	cause-and-effect diagrams, mind maps(Idea 37 on p. 52) comparing and contrasting – tables, Venn diagrams
Ordering and ranking	ladders and pyramids
Concluding and evaluating	living graphs (Idea 50 on p. 71)

Primary colleagues may be more familiar with working walls than secondary practitioners, yet they have relevance for learners at every key stage. They are generally used to provide a stimulus at the beginning of a topic or be a focus for new material as the topic develops over time.

Identify a large, accessible space in the classroom to position your working wall. To start a topic, you may want to prepare a snappy title and a series of key questions. Early on, ask learners to contribute their own subquestions; you may want to change these regularly as the topic progresses.

Dedicate an area to the scaffolding of language elements pertinent to the topic. Build up key words or phrases over time; you may want to start a new topic by eliciting some suggestions from the class. Additionally, you will want to include talk or writing prompts that model the type of language that you expect to be used by learners in specific activities, such as in presentations and in fiction or non-fiction writing. Where possible, provide multilingual versions of important key words or phrases.

To reinforce learning, make thoughtful use of significant images and key visuals (Idea 38 on p. 53) such as timelines, maps, scientific models, mind maps (Idea 37 on p. 52).

Working Walls

The internet can be a bewildering place for learners, particularly those still acquiring full academic proficiency in English. Not only are there likely to be numerous sources, but the quality, reliability and level of language will all affect the usefulness of the information. For this reason it can be a good idea to prepare a limited list of appropriate websites for a particular topic or activity. This will help EAL learners who may otherwise waste a lot of time on irrelevant or inaccessible information.

Utilizing effective search techniques will help EAL learners because successful searches generally produce a smaller numbers of web-page returns with a better match to the initial keywords.

Here are some recommended tips and tricks. Ensure that learners:

- limit the number of keywords used for searching;
- don't use high frequency words as part of their searches;
- check that words are spelled correctly;
- avoid subject-specific words with double meanings, as searching with them will return irrelevant information;
- review the number of page results; lower numbers are generally good;
- know how to use advanced search techniques; for example,
  o using logical operators to refine searches: '+'; '-' or 'not'; 'and'; 'or'; and the like;
  o searching for specific phrases by, for example, encapsulating them in inverted commas;
  o customizing searches by reading level; for example, search web pages for a 'basic' reading level;
- understand that it may be appropriate to use ability in L1 to search for and access information in a preferred language.

Wikipedia is a perfect example of the quandary of using internet-based sources. Reliability of information can be a particular issue because of the way the content has been authored. In addition, inappropriate use is likely to be more confusing than useful for many EAL learners. However, when used correctly, Wikipedia can be an invaluable research tool. Generally, Wikipedia should be restricted to older learners because of the sophistication of both language and concepts.

Where possible, some EAL learners will be able to search for and read articles in a potentially stronger L1. Many articles written in English have a corresponding version in another language. When a similar article in another language is available, it often becomes available as a link from the English article. While not direct translations, they may cover similar content and have been quality assured.

Another useful feature for EAL learners is that many linked articles have been written in simpler English and, when available, can be accessed again from the main article.

USEFUL RESOURCE

'Simple English' version of Wikipedia – www.simple.
wikipedia.org/

Wikipedia

Pre-teaching relevant academic language before exposing EAL learners to the main content of a lesson has been shown to be a successful strategy. It helps learners overcome the double challenge of encountering new content alongside the language demands of the specific task.

Focused preparatory language teaching is best delivered during short-term withdrawal sessions or in out-of-hours clubs. Additionally, you could notify parents or carers of upcoming work so that they can prepare their children at home.

However pre-teaching is organized, it is important that learners encounter new language within a clear curriculum-related context in order for meaning to be made explicit. In addition, the key language will be best acquired when they can repeatedly see, hear and read new words in order to write them in sentences and apply them in new situations. Academic language should include key vocabulary, oft-repeated sentence structures and specific connectives; particular attention should be given to preparing learners for writing within different genres, in a particular register and according to the conventions of specific text types.

Pre-teaching new language should be fun and interactive. Try any of these tools and ideas:

- language flashcards;
- word or sentence dominoes;
- word searches or crosswords supported by visuals;
- labelling key visuals;
- barrier games on a particular topic (Idea 58 on p. 84); bingo – words matched to definitions (Idea 44 on p. 59); paragraph puzzles – where text has been chopped up into words, phrases or whole sentences;
- follow me' activities (Idea 44 on p. 59);
- sorting words or phrases into graphic organizers (Idea 39 on p. 54);
- dictogloss (Idea 49 on p. 69); and Socratic talk (Idea 63 on p. 91);

The following are a few ideas for reinforcing and recapping recently acquired language.

Prepare a set of 'connection cards' ready for a language-based starter activity. Connection cards are matching pairs, pairs that go together: vocabulary and definitions, top and tail sentences, cause-and-effect statements. Give learners a connection card each, and encourage them to find the matching card. At the end of a set time period, get each learner pair to read out their matched cards to check that they are correct.

A bingo starter activity is an excellent way to recap key language in preparation for the main lesson activity. Create a set of bingo cards based upon key vocabulary and a set of definitions to read out during the bingo activity. Play the game until someone 'wins'. Go through each definition to ensure the key words are matched correctly.

'Follow me' is a card-based oral activity that is particularly useful for learners who are beginning to read, as the activity has a simple script from which to work. Each learner is given one card; the idea is that one learner starts by reading out the card, which might say something such as 'I have a square, how many lines of symmetry do I have?' In this case the learner with the card that says 'I have four; tell me another shape with four right angles' should read it out, and so on. Each card should have only one following card to avoid any confusion.

To recap learning at the end of a lesson, try the 'generation game' activity. Prepare a PowerPoint visual containing all the language elements and other information relevant to a particular topic. Convey each idea on its own slide using appropriate text, images and sounds. Set the presentation to play automatically, so that each slide remains on screen for a set amount of time before giving way to the next. When the presentation is over, ask learners to try and remember as many pieces of language or information as possible.

USEFUL SOFTWARE

Formulator Tarsia – http://www.mmlsoft.com/index. php?option=com_content&task=view&id=9&Itemid=10

Reinforcing and Recapping Language

The Mathematics Problem

Mathematics provides a good example of the importance of teaching language (Ideas 43–44 on pp. 58–59); alongside curriculum content. There is evidence that many EAL learners, as well as their monolingual peers, underachieve because the UK mathematics curriculum has significant language demands. Specific ideas include the following:

- provide plenty of opportunity to talk about mathematics – for example, try the Talking Maths programme (Idea 98 on p. 145); show learners how to break wordy problems down into manageable chunks;
- focus on academic vocabulary – for example, the many different terms for each numerical operator;
- create mathematical calligrams to reinforce learning; associate a shape or picture with a word;
- highlight language anomalies: homophones such as 'sine' and 'sign'; homonyms like 'mean', 'power', 'root', which have several different meanings.

Many learners who have studied mathematics abroad are gifted mathematicians, but have additional cultural hurdles to overcome before they can demonstrate their true ability. They may have learned some areas (e.g., algebra, trigonometry) in significant depth, yet will have missed other topics completely – for example, investigative mathematics. Here are some other issues that may need attention:

- See whether learners are familiar with the Hindu-Arabic numerals, as they may have used other number systems in their country of origin.
- Clarify how decimal points, multiplication signs and other symbols differ in their use from country to country.
- If they are secure, encourage learners to use their own way of solving number problems; note that some methods may be very different to those taught in UK schools.

- In some cultures, learners rely upon one secure method of solving a problem and may find it difficult to understand the notion of trying alternative methods.

Mathematical Calligram

USEFUL RESOURCE
www.collaborativelearning.org/mathsonline.html

Integrated Approaches to Learning

Digital Storytelling – Running a Project

Digital storytelling is a perfect way to integrate skills from across the curriculum. Essentially a digital story is a recorded narrative involving speech, music, text and visual elements, which are usually bound together in a video-based format.

Plan projects that span several sessions over the course of a week, or try collapsing the timetable into a whole day. Decide on a theme – for example, traditional tales, stories from other cultures, personal narratives, biographies of famous people, re-enactments of historical events.

It is critical to create well-balanced groups where EAL learners can work alongside confident English speakers. There is a real opportunity here to activate prior learning by encouraging EAL learners to share stories from their own backgrounds and perform retellings in their own language as well as English.

Once a theme has been chosen, the next step involves storyboarding. Ask the groups to split the narrative into six to eight sections. Provide a template for them to illustrate with drawings and annotations what is happening in each scene. The group will also need to decide on a technique for packaging the story; for example, freeze-frame photographs, video, puppets or clay animation. Provide a slot of time to allow the group to source additional things like clothing, props and digital sounds or music.

Narration for each section of the story should be kept to a minimum. Experience shows that best results are achieved by writing the narration down and ensuring that learners have plenty of time to rehearse. Record audio separately from the visual element; this particularly benefits shy EAL learners who prefer to prepare their oral contribution somewhere private. Encourage them to review their efforts and re-record where necessary. Provide opportunities to use L1 as well.

Narration, music, visuals and text can be bound together using a range of software: Photo Story 3 (Idea 47 on p. 66), PowerPoint, Movie Maker and the like.

Organize a showcase at the end so everyone can see all
the finished versions. Make sure you keep copies on disc
or the school's VLE, and use them for assessment
purposes.

USEFUL RESOURCE

Digital storytelling – http://digitalstorytelling.segfl.org.uk/

Digital Storytelling – Using Photo Story 3

Photo Story 3 is free software. It is perfect for digital storytelling because it is simple enough to be used by very young learners, yet it features more sophisticated tools for secondary-age learners. Photo Story allows a user to tell a story by animating a sequence of images alongside music and oral narration.

A Photo Story project usually involves a group of learners taking a number of digital photographs as the basis for the story; additional images can be found on the internet or scanned from printed sources. Images work best in landscape mode, so ensure digital photos and other images are prepared in this orientation.

Here are some ideas for different types of projects.

- Freeze-frame. The group re-enacts a story through a series of still photographs. Different settings around the school need to be identified, although learners may be able to paint large backgrounds or even stand in front of an image on the IWB. The group will also need to source appropriate clothes and props.
- Still images using toys or puppets. The toys or puppets will need to 'act' in front of a home-made stage, or the group can hold the 'characters' in front of a computer screen displaying a relevant picture.
- Model or sandtray (photos of inanimate objects placed within different scenes to illustrate the main events of the story). Characters can be sourced from toy miniatures, Playmobil or Lego or made from clay or plasticine. The group could hand-paint backdrops or use printed photographs.
- Scanned storybook images. Here the artwork becomes the visual element.
- Mixed-media approach. Sequencing images might include real photographs, paintings, cartoons, signs or symbols to create a narrative.

At their simplest, talking books are fiction or non-fiction texts with images and some form of audio-based component. They can be physical or electronic in form; some can be purchased, and many can be downloaded for free from the internet or created using software tools.

Using and creating talking books is a powerful way to seamlessly integrate speaking, listening, reading and writing with the creative arts, alongside cross-curricular use of ICT. There can be particular benefits for EAL learners, especially if they can draw upon traditional stories or life experiences from their own cultural background and when they can utilize expertise in their L1 to produce multi-language versions.

Making talking books works best within the mainstream classroom, although it can also be successful in withdrawal intervention sessions (Idea 21 on p. 35). Organize learners into small groups, where EAL learners work alongside peers who can model good use of English. The informal talk that is generated during group work will be particularly beneficial for beginner EAL learners. In addition, the more formal literacy demands of reading and writing new texts, perhaps with L1 translation, will help more advanced EAL learners.

Inspiration for cross-cultural bilingual stories can be elicited from learners. Many publishers stock a good range of texts – for example, Mantra Lingua and Milet. There are also many useful sites on the internet, including the International Children's Digital Library (http://en.childrenslibrary.org/).

There are many tools to produce multilingual talking books.

- Microsoft Power Point (or a similar application), where text, graphics and audio content can be embedded together on different slides to depict the ideas of a 'virtual' book.
- 2Simple's 2Create-a-story is great for early years.

- Immersive Education's Kar2ouche is particularly useful for non-fiction texts.
- Cricksoft's Clicker (Idea 77 on p. 112).
- Printed texts and graphic 'novels', combined with Mantra Lingua's Talking Stickers (Idea 60 on p. 87).

USEFUL RESOURCE

More information can be found at www.youtube.com/watch?v=VSgHU34tYmg.

This activity is an excellent way to link active listening, note taking and writing alongside curriculum delivery. It supports the acquisition of language – including vocabulary, typical phrases and connectives – and types of writing that are distinctive to particular subjects. In a Dictogloss activity, a text is read several times to learners working in small groups. As the activity progresses, the groups work collaboratively to piece together a similar but not identical version of the original text. While this may sound like dictation, be assured that it is not the same.

PREPARATION

The chosen text needs to be relatively short and should focus upon specific content and language elements that you wish to reinforce. Ensure each group has a mixture of EAL learners and orally proficient English speakers. It can help to provide the participants with a note-taking graphic organizer (Idea 39 on p. 54). that suits the text type.

RUNNING THE ACTIVITY

1. Read the text aloud at normal speed and encourage each group to listen without taking notes; then briefly ask them to explain the gist of the text.
2. Read the text a second time, slightly more slowly; allow learners to take notes with an emphasis on more obvious elements, like facts and specific vocabulary.
3. Read the text a third time; continue note taking, but this time devote more attention to specific phrases and connectives that link ideas together.
4. Finally, allow —ten to fifteen minutes for the groups to piece together as much of the text as possible.

SUMMING-UP

Choose several groups to read their collaboratively developed texts aloud and draw out specific points, such as which elements were easy to recreate and which were more difficult. This should help inform a focus for future work.

USEFUL RESOURCE

DCSF (2009), Ensuring the attainment of more advanced learners of EAL – CPD 5: Bridging talk and text – http://nationalstrategies.standards.dcsf.gov.uk/ downloader/f25345cd45fbf047227eded62438b72a. pdf

Analysing and evaluating data is a form of higher-order thinking that is difficult for some EAL learners to fully express through writing. An explanatory text needs a specific structure and utilizes cause-and-effect language and a range of technical vocabulary pertinent to different subject areas. Use 'living graphs' to help learners interpret trends and patterns in data that have been obtained through their own investigations or with graphs drawn from pre-existing data.

Living graphs require learners to justify the position of information against a timeline of events. In preparation, create a variety of true statements that help to describe and explain the overall shape of the graph. Try to include ambiguous or irrelevant information, as this encourages active reading. Produce a set of cards containing all the statements, and encourage learners to place them in appropriate positions on the graph. Encourage the group to discard any irrelevant statements.

Living graphs can be developed around any kind of continuous data; for example,

- a bar graph showing how the volume of traffic varies over the course of a day;
- a seismograph of earth movements before, during and after an earthquake;
- a population pyramid illustrating population demographics over time;
- a line graph describing the interrelationship between a predator and its prey over a number of years.

Once the position of the statements has been agreed, learners can sequence them to form a detailed, cohesive piece of writing – for example, an explanation of how the flow of traffic changes throughout the day.

Blogs and Tweets

Social networking tools are familiar to most learners who were born in the United Kingdom, and you may also discover that this is the case for many new-arrival learners. Some will not have had this experience and will need a little time to adjust.

Getting learners involved in blogging is an excellent way of linking reading and writing, as well as developing learners' media-literacy skills. Try to devise activities that require learners to write about issues from their own point of view or, alternatively, in a more factual, impartial way. Encourage learners to read each other's blogs and add their own comments, as this can be highly motivating for them. Most VLEs support blogs as well as Edmodo and a plethora of other secure educational sites.

Twitter is a micro-blogging tool that allows a user to communicate short messages (called tweets) of up to 140 characters to a nominated group of individuals. Its ease of use and restriction on message length is proving popular among educators working with learners acquiring English. By its very nature, Twitter requires learners to think about the formality of their communication, as well as about how to write concisely.

It makes sense to set up a unique Twitter account just for use with a particular group or class of learners. Using this account you will be able to initiate many different kinds of collaborative reading and writing tasks, including:

- researching definitions of new words through a 'word of the week' activity;
- writing a summary of the last lesson;
- improving a sentence by changing or adding just one word at a time;
- building a collaborative story by taking turns at contributing to it;
- tweeting from the perspective of a historical character or celebrity;
- organizing a poll or vote about a specific subject.

USEFUL RESOURCES
Twitter – http://twitter.com/
Edmodo – www.edmodo.com/

Build a Wiki

Essentially, a wiki is a website that anyone can read and edit. As such, wikis develop in a collaborative way, through a number of revisions before a final version. Using wikis within the curriculum is a great way to reinforce concepts and knowledge within a subject area, as well as linking all four strands of English. This type of activity suits more advanced learners of EAL – because learners need to use more formal or academic language – and requires them to have reasonable comprehension and editing skills.

Most school VLEs have a module that allows for building wikis; there are also many free solutions available on the internet. Develop an idea for a wiki within your subject area: creating topic vocabulary definitions, analysing a book or play, producing a how-to guide, critiquing a famous painting or composition, writing a travel brochure or the like.

You will need to have an introductory session where learners are shown how to use all the wiki tools. They need to understand that wikis develop over time and that there is usually an initial draft that undergoes a series of edits. Initially, it helps to group learners together so they can work collaboratively on a specific section of the wiki. For the first draft, this allows for plenty of discussion and debate and captures a range of ideas. Next, allow groups to review each other's drafts, and begin the editing process. During this stage, it is important to stress the importance of being sensitive to the writing produced by other learners. They need to be encouraged to prune writing and to look for more formal and academic ways of expressing information. A final proofreading stage should concentrate on checking the accuracy of information, correcting spelling and grammar and ensuring a consistent style.

Once the wiki is published, you may want to get other classes to evaluate it. Developing a rubric for this purpose can be helpful. Keep the wiki for posterity; it may prove useful as an information source for future learners as well as be a model to show the next class that comes to do a similar task.

Webquests encourage an enquiry-based approach to finding information on the internet. Through a number of significant questions, learners are guided towards specific websites that require them to gather, synthesize and repurpose information in a new form. Since they enable a practitioner to link speaking and listening and reading and writing alongside cognitively demanding activities, they are very suitable for more advanced EAL learners.

Start by defining the body of information that will be revealed. You will need to identify suitable websites and ensure that the language-level is appropriate for the class. It helps to formulate a number of leading questions to guide information retrieval, and you will need to specify what learners need to do with the information they find. Consider grouping learners so they can talk about the task, perhaps using a KWL grid to capture their thoughts (KWL: What I *k*now, what I *w*ant to know, what I have *l*earned).

In a geographical context, learners might be asked to use the internet to learn about another country. If this were the totality of the activity, it would not be a webquest because it lacked a clear focus. In a webquest, different tasks need to lead to a significant end point, one where information has been processed, evaluated and used in another context. In line with Bloom's Taxonomy (Idea 23 on p. 38). and depths of critical thinking, a range of increasingly demanding tasks might include the following:

- evaluate: peer review other groups' travel brochures;
- synthesize: acquire knowledge and record interesting information about the country from a number of websites;
- analyse: research the features of travel brochures on the internet;
- apply: use information to plan and create a travel brochure;
- comprehend: sift information for relevance;

Webquests

- create knowledge: write a persuasive letter encouraging people to visit the country.

Designing your own webquest is always the best course of action, but it is perfectly possible to find suitable ones all over the internet.

Encouraging Speaking and Listening

Effective Questioning Techniques

A perennial worry for many practitioners is the lack of interaction by EAL learners during teacher-led discussions, especially in whole-class situations. This can be true for both beginner and advanced learners. While recognizing that it is important to respect an initial silent phase for those new to English, before long such learners should be taking part along with their peers.

Here are some useful tips to encourage all learners to participate in oral discussions.

- Establish a culture that encourages all learners to take risks without the worry of being wrong.
- Employ the use of mini-whiteboards and visual feedback systems (Idea 8 on p. 15); these enable reticent talkers to participate visually at first, encouraging more oral contribution in the future.
- Initiate a 'no hands up' rule, allowing you to control who attempts to answer questions.
- Avoid closed questions that require yes/no or single-word answers, except for complete beginners who you feel sure will benefit from getting the answer correct in front of their peers.
- Utilize more open-ended questions that require greater detail or that have a number of possible answers; these questions give learners more opportunity to show what they do and don't know.
- Try to avoid using idiomatic language which is very hard for most EAL learners to understand.
- Give learners plenty of thinking time prior to a response.
- Encourage learners to discuss the question in pairs or groups of three, providing an opportunity to rehearse answers; group EAL learners appropriately (Idea 20 on p. 34).
- Where individuals and groups need to report back in turn, allow beginners to take their turn later in the sequence so that they can hear answers being modelled by their peers.

The multi-modal nature of drama makes it an effective tool for supporting the acquisition of oral skills, as well as for teaching learners about themselves and the wider world. It has most impact when it is embedded across the curriculum and used in imaginative ways to consolidate learning. Drama offers a range of supports for making meaning clear; visual, audio, kinaesthetic and practitioner modelling. When learners work collaboratively, they will not only develop colloquial language during the planning stages but also a more academic formal style when orally presenting. It helps to allow less confident EAL learners perform early but not first, so that they can learn from watching the first few groups. Watching performance helps to reinforce turn taking and active listening.

Sometimes you may organize a whole-class dramatic technique that can benefit new-to-English learners, as they can model themselves on others and avoid feeling too conspicuous. Examples in different subjects include asking learners to behave like particles in liquid or encouraging learners to mark the moment of a story using freeze-frames and thought tracks to illustrate how a character is feeling at a specific plot point. Organizing the group into a human orchestra to produce a soundscape can allow the teacher to create a specific atmosphere – for example, of a moment in a novel, a historical location or a rainforest – using only voice and body percussion. This allows teachers a rich starting point to build an imagined picture that can be drawn upon through discussion tasks and later on in their written work.

The enhanced language demands of a more individualized strategy such as hot-seating may be more appropriate for advanced EAL learners. This activity requires one or more learners to adopt the personality of a character or object. The learner in the hot seat needs as much information about the character as possible. The information may have been taught to the whole class over the course of a few weeks or it may be given solely to the individual immediately prior to the activity. The rest of the class develops suitable questions that the character or object in the hot seat answers, using imagination and building upon an understanding of the subject.

It is well established that some learners need additional support for certain kinds of writing – for example, writing frames (Idea 70 on p. 102). However, it is also true that those learners who are emerging from a silent phase or who are reticent speakers will benefit from scaffolding to support talk. Talk prompts are designed to encourage learners to participate in a range of different oral contexts.

In order to encourage learners to participate in class discussions, group work and presentations, it is a good idea to have oral prompts available in an easily accessible format. Some learners will be able to read and use simple written forms, whereas others may require digitally recorded versions for example, through RecorderPENs and talking labels (Idea 60 on p. 87). or podcasts distributed through the school's VLE.

At their simplest, they are open-ended sentence starters and commonly use phrases designed to prompt colloquial language needed for collaborative activities. For example, playing a board game:

> It's your/my turn.
> Roll the dice.
> Move . . . spaces.
> Pick up a card.

Curriculum-related talk prompts aim to scaffold the development of more formal or presentational language. They tend to include more sophisticated sentence structures and connectives and may include key vocabulary; for example, for-and-against arguments:

> I think that . . .
> I agree/disagree with . . . because
> Other reasons include . . .
> Also/additionally . . .
> To conclude . . .

For children new to English, board games and similar activities are perfect for generating both colloquial (BICs) and more academic (CALP) language in a familiar context. Board games work on many levels and help to develop important skills:

- logic and strategy;
- cooperation and turn taking;
- speaking and especially listening;
- repetitive language – vocabulary and short phrases;
- academic language (when curriculum-based).

Small-group withdrawal intervention sessions:

1. Choose any well-known traditional multi-player board game with simple rules. This is an excellent opportunity for EAL learners to teach their peers a game that comes from their own cultural background.
2. Select a target group of beginner EAL learners and one or more articulate English speakers.
3. Support with an additional adult.
4. Provide game-playing oral prompt sheets where necessary (Idea 56 on p. 81).

In the classroom

- As above.
- Create and use a game based upon the curriculum; for example, a topic, storybook or play script.

It is also an excellent idea to enable groups to create their own board games, particularly when related to the curriculum. Speaking and listening naturally happens when children collaborate on creating the rules and making the board and other props. More advanced EAL learners can also help to write the rules and other text, such as question cards. Recordable TalkingPENs and stickers (Idea 60 on p. 87) can also be used to add an oral element to the game.

Finally, encourage the groups to swap games and play and evaluate them.

Racing to English has a useful set of printable board games that focus on developing speaking and listening, together with some blank templates to develop your own games.

USEFUL RESOURCE

Racing to English – www.racingtoenglish.co.uk/

Barrier Games

Particularly useful for children and young people at the early stages of learning English, barrier games focus on developing speaking and listening skills. Barrier games can also help to develop instructional language, question starters, use of present tense, positional vocabulary, comparative terms, descriptive terminology and subject-specific language.

Typically, in barrier games information is conveyed orally between two players. Position each participant on either side of a physical barrier to prevent them from seeing an object that one or the other possesses. Ensure they can communicate easily, both orally and through non-verbal cues. One participant provides a detailed description of a 'resource' that they have been given or made themselves, and the other participant must recreate it as accurately as possible. This could be a drawing, an object or a sequence of items. Resources can be selected from any subject; they function best when linked to work currently occurring in the mainstream curriculum.

Sometimes, in a barrier game a pair of learners work together to complete a visual resource from different versions that they both possess. As each learner holds information that the other needs, they must work collaboratively to piece together a complete version. Each learner takes turns to ask questions in order to obtain missing information on their resource. Questions tend to focus on visual details: size, position, shape, colour, amount and written information such as text and numbers. For example, *What is next to . . . ? What colour is . . . ? Is it larger than . . . ? How many . . . ?* The resources should be similar to each other but with a number of significant omissions. Obviously every omission on one resource must be visible on the other. Visual resources that work well for this type of activity include maps, diagrams, graphs, paintings, tables of information and timelines.

Sometimes it can be useful to pair learners up on either side of the barrier so they can discuss their questions and answers, especially if a beginner EAL learner is paired with an orally more proficient peer. A practitioner's input will also help keep participants on task.

Talking Devices

These digital products allow playback and recording of audio files to support speaking and listening across the curriculum. Being able to hear professionally recorded speech provides instant access to curriculum-related information and effective language models.

The best feature of talking devices is being able to record speech, as well as music, ambient sounds and other oral elements. Plan activities that require EAL learners to record a conversation, their thoughts about an area of learning or a reading sample. Encourage them to listen to their recordings, look for errors and re-record if necessary. Use the recording function as a talk-for-writing approach where pairs and small groups can revisit conversations as a support for the writing process. Recording can also support assessment-for-learning (AfL) and assessing-pupil-progress (APP) activities; progress in speaking and listening can be monitored over time.

Recordable devices like Talking tins or postcards are simple to use and have many applications across the curriculum. Practitioner and/or EAL learners can use them to plan individual or collaborative stories or non-fiction writing. They can be used to develop treasure trails, create vocabulary prompts, design knowledge puzzles and support learning of phonemes and word building or segmenting.

Talking photo albums are perfect for linking visuals with audio elements. Use them to support new-arrival induction; for example, learners can build personal scrap books or life stories using carefully selected printed images alongside recorded narration – this could be in L1 or English. They could develop talking books from familiar stories or perhaps make a book about their new school. Alternatively, allow the new learner to use it as a diary to record thoughts and images of their first few weeks at school.

USEFUL RESOURCES

TTS-Group – www.tts-group.co.uk/
Talking Products – www.talkingproducts.com/

PENPal™ is a pointing device that can play audio files when a user touches the tip of the pen to prepared hot spots on printed surfaces. There are many audio-enabled resources that work with the device, such as bilingual books and curriculum-related charts. However, the PENpal™ can also record audio and link the sound file to a sticky label that can be affixed to any surface. This enables practitioners to make bespoke resources for learners; it also allows learners to sound-enable their work and to create talking games or exhibits.

As a practitioner you will be able to make differentiated materials to scaffold learning at different levels. Leave instructions, hints and key vocabulary or phrases on help cards, texts and worksheets to support a learning task. Secure the use of a bilingual practitioner to create support materials in L1. Leave oral feedback on work for learners who cannot read your comments, and use the pen to communicate with the home, by sending oral messages back and forth overnight. Make L1 oral translations of school forms to help with new-arrival induction.

In the hands of learners, the PENpal™ becomes the focus for speaking and listening activities. Allow beginner EAL learners to produce oral versions of work if the more formal written demand is beyond their current skill level. Develop activities for learners that require them to work together to develop sound-enabled products – for example, talking board or card games, help sheets and talking books. Make a class talking photo album, where the class can introduce itself to a new learner, or make a talking yearbook. Develop whole-school initiatives, such as creating an interactive talking display about the nationalities and language skills of all the learners and adults at the school.

USEFUL RESOURCE
Mantra Lingua's PENpal™ – www.mantralingua.com/

Recordable Talkingpen (Penpal™)

If you are having trouble with encouraging EAL learners to talk in class, particularly in more formal situations, then Voki can help. This online tool allows a user to create a customized character (avatar) that can 'read' text aloud or 'speak' it from an audio recording. The creative process is very motivating for learners and can really encourage them to participate in any subsequent oral task.

To begin with, encourage reticent speakers to work with Voki's text-to-speech voice synthesizer. Working on individual or collaboratively developed texts, the user types or pastes text into the system and chooses from a range of different voices. Hearing good-quality audio rendering of the text provides an effective model, helping learners to spot mistakes and rehearse for their own recordings.

Eventually learners will have the confidence to do their own recording. Some may prefer to record an oral version away from the computer and import it into the system at a later time. Provide a quiet space and portable recording equipment for them. Some learners will want privacy, while others may appreciate the presence of supportive peers. Another way of preparing the audio is to attach a microphone to the computer and record directly into Voki. When the audio has been linked to the avatar, the whole Voki can be exported and saved to a website or embedded in a blog or VLE.

Voki is an excellent tool for preparing learners for oral presentations: show and tell, storytelling, public speaking and so on. Since finished versions can be stored as evidence, the tool can be used to assess speaking and listening. It may also be useful to compare Vokis produced at the beginning of the year and at the end in order to show progress over time.

USEFUL RESOURCE
Voki – www.voki.com/

This is another effective activity to encourage speaking and listening in preparation for a piece of argumentative or persuasive writing. A simple version of the technique requires you to pose a question or statement that is likely to promote a range of views in the class. In small groups, encourage learners to come to a consensus about where to place the question or statement along an opinion-line continuum (as below).

Once the question or statement has been positioned, ask a representative from one group to indicate where they placed it along the opinion line and to justify their decision with reasons. Encourage the rest of the class to offer supportive comments or counter-arguments where appropriate. It can be useful for a practitioner to model this type of talk to the class, and it may also help to provide some EAL learners with talk prompt sheets (Idea 56 on p. 81) to help with scaffolding oral contributions.

This activity also works well with multiple statements around a particular theme. Allow each group the option to choose a statement that feels significant to them; alternatively, allocate each group a different statement.

In a suitable room, you might like to run the activity more kinaesthetically. Again, start the activity as a paper-based group task by posing one or more questions or statements. Place five large opinion signs along one of the walls, and ask a representative from each group to stand in the appropriate position. Next, ask each representative to justify the chosen position, and allow the rest of the class to support or counter-argue where necessary. If the group members change their mind following the class discussion, then the representative can move to a new position.

USEFUL RESOURCE

DfES (2009). 'Ensuring the attainment of more advanced learners of English as an additional language: CPD modules'. CPDM4 –Talk as a tool for thinking.

In a Socratic talk exercise a group of learners observe a discussion or debate surrounding a central question or idea in order for all participants to learn from and comment on the nature of exploratory talk. As the activity proceeds, different points of view about a topic are modelled in a way that helps participants think through their ideas and has the added benefit of introducing and reinforcing key concepts and vocabulary pertinent to the curriculum topic being studied.

A Socratic activity is appropriate for all kinds of learners, but it has been shown to have particular benefits for advanced EAL learners.

PREPARATION

The content of the activity can be drawn for any curriculum area but works best when there is one main question for consideration; for example, *'Is Damien Hirst a good artist?'* or *'Was Columbus a hero or a villain?'* It helps to have one or more pieces of media to consider, such as samples of writing, diagrams or images. Briefing the group that will be conducting the discussion or debate and giving them time to collect their thoughts is a good idea. Set up the room with oral participants in a central area and the observers around the outside; the inner group should comprise orally confident learners. Provide each observer with a different cue card that asks them to listen for one specific feature; for example, *'Write down any examples of the use of key vocabulary'* or *'How do participants show that they agree with a point of view? Write down some examples.'*

THE DISCUSSION OR DEBATE

Remind observers of the task on their cue cards; remind them, too, that they must remain silent throughout. Allow the discussion or debate to continue for between 5 and 10 minutes. As a practitioner, only intervene if the

Socratic Talk – Talk as a Tool for Thinking

conversation is flagging or one person begins to dominates the conversation

REVIEW

Ask an observer to read out the task on the cue card. Allow him or her to feedback the findings. Draw other observers in where appropriate. Repeat until satisfied that the key points have emerged.

This type of activity is excellent for helping learners to:

- understand the importance of listening;
- develop speaking strategies, such as how to disagree without causing offence;
- organize their thoughts prior to follow-up activities like presentations and writing tasks; for example, 'writing to inform, explain and describe' and 'writing to argue, persuade and advise'.

USEFUL RESOURCE

DfES (2009). 'Ensuring the attainment of more advanced learners of English as an additional language: CPD modules'. CPDM4 – Talk as a tool for thinking.

Developing Reading

Use of Bilingual Texts

Remembering that not all EAL learners or parents are literate in L1, bilingual texts can have a significant role to play in activating a learner's prior knowledge, as well as supporting their access to the curriculum.

For new-to-English learners, a bilingual storybook provides instant access to a story that can inform subsequent literacy tasks, whether in English or another language. Bilingual learners beyond the early stages of learning English will benefit from exposure to both texts at the same time. Sometimes, try covering one of the texts or particular words or phrases for more active reading. In this way bilingual learners will be able to transfer knowledge over from L1 to English and vice versa.

All learners will benefit from being able to see two different scripts on the same page. Get groups to compare specific elements such as text directionality, word breaks and punctuation, and ask them to identify root words that may be common to the two languages.

Get the family on board. Develop guidance for parents about how to share a book with their child and translate it into the main community languages. Helpful guidance for engaging parents can be obtained from the publication entitled 'Developing reading skills through home languages'.

USEFUL RESOURCES

'Developing reading skills through home languages' –
http://emat.redbridge.lgfl.digitalbrain.com/lgfl/leas/
redbridge/schools/emat/web/EAL/DevRdgSkillsOrder/
UEL Dual-language Books – www.uel.ac.uk/education/
research/duallanguagebooks/

Choosing appropriate reading material can be extremely challenging. It is all too easy to choose texts that are too demanding or ones which are simplistic and demeaning to the age and cognitive ability of the EAL learner.

Ensure that texts are well produced with clear fonts and well-chosen illustrations that add contextual meaning. Stories with strong narratives or familiar non-fiction topics will be more appealing than texts without an authentic purpose. Similarly, learners are more likely to engage with texts that relate to their own experiences, reflect the society in which they live and deal with issues of culture and religion sensitively, challenging bias and stereotype where necessary.

Try to select stories that are written with an active voice, as this will be more accessible to EAL learners who will mostly be drawing from their experiences in oral communication. Avoid texts that are overly colloquial, as this type of language tends to lie outside the experience of many EAL learners, particularly beginners. Where texts contain an abundance of academic and technical language, choose those that provide vocabulary explanations.

Choosing Appropriate Texts

Graphic Readers

Suitable books should be identified for those at the early stages of reading. It is really important to ensure that the level of language is challenging while at the same time ensuring that the content is cognitively and culturally suitable for the age and maturity of the learner.

Graphic readers present fiction (and sometimes non-fiction) through a more visual cartoon style than traditional books do. Text tends to be more informal, supported visually through stylistic conventions and images that help convey meaning. Many also contain vocabulary and grammar activities linked to the text.

Many EAL learners, including those from abroad, may be familiar with cartoons (for example manga). However, it is still important to explain some of the more immediate conventions; for example, reading directionality; how text is organized to imply narrative, thoughts and speech; and the meaning of onomatopoeic expressions, ellipses and other unusual punctuation.

Visual cues can also be confusing. You could prepare learners by asking them to think of ways to visually communicate ideas without any words; for example, speed, a bad smell, heat, cold, a ringing telephone, anger, fear or confusion.

Here are some other ideas for developing active reading:

- Text marking – identify time connectives, setting description, powerful verbs and so on;
- Cloze procedure – blank individual words that need to be predicted;
- Text reconstruction – remove chunks of text from narrative panes or speech or thought bubbles, and ask learners to rewrite small sections using their own words;
- Story sequence – provide a scrambled set of panes that require sequencing to retell the story;
- Comic jigsaw – separate all the text from the images and ask learners to recombine them correctly.

Graphic Shakespeare
Oxford Dominoes Series
Raintree graphic novels

DARTs are designed to challenge learners to engage with texts by using active reading strategies. Some DARTs activities help learners consider the overall structure of a text, while others focus on supporting understanding and interpretation. Choosing the right one to meet the learning needs of the learners is critical. They can be used effectively across the curriculum with fiction and non-fiction texts.

At their simplest, activities such as gap-fill exercises, top-and-tail sentences and sentence halves and jumbled sentences or paragraphs will benefit EAL learners. Learners need to look carefully for keywords and logical connectives to complete or recreate the text. To improve writing structure, get learners to demarcate one long paragraph that has no full stops. For non-fiction texts such as report writing, ask learners to break up an unformatted piece of text using topic sentences and headings or sub-headings. Either provide those headings or encourage learners to create their own.

Another useful strategy is to ask learners to mark important words in preparation for further tasks – for example, highlighting 'weak' verbs in order to identify where to use more powerful ones. Learners sometimes struggle to choose the right connective to signpost their writing effectively. In argumentative writing, encourage learners to text-mark all the connectives and choose more suitable words to mark where additional points are being made as opposed to making counter-arguments.

When working with texts from different sources, marking words or phrases in different colours can help organize ideas and language conceptually prior to repurposing text into a different format. Once text is categorized, provide learners with graphic organizers (Idea 39 on p. 54); this will help them to part-process chunks of language before transforming it into, say, a letter, newspaper article or advertisement.

It is not uncommon for learners of EAL to demonstrate greater proficiency with spoken language than they can through their reading or writing in English. Screen-reading software, which can be used to read text aloud to a user, enables learners to access written information that would otherwise be inaccessible to them.

It is a good idea to have screen readers installed on various computers around the school. Some versions work within word processors and web browsers, while others allow text to be pasted from the clipboard. There are also portable versions that need no installation and can be accessed directly from a memory stick.

Experiment by choosing appropriately synthesized voices and other software settings. Some screen readers allow a user to change the speed of oral reading; this can assist learners with differing linguistic and cognitive abilities. It may also be possible to set up the software to highlight text as it is read aloud; doing this helps to reinforce word recognition.

USEFUL RESOURCE

Recommended screen-reading software: Read Please 2003 – www.readplease.com/

Screen-Reading Software

Speech-Recognition Technology

A number of online reading schemes currently employ speech-recognition technology. Enrolling learners within these programmes can be extremely beneficial in terms of improving their decoding skills. This technology can help learners with both pronunciation and, more specifically, word recognition. Reading schemes that employ speech recognition enable learners to compare their efforts against standard oral versions, helping them to spot repeated errors. In addition the software can track a learner's progress, highlighting specific mistakes and suggesting areas for improvement.

Note that stand-alone speech-recognition software that requires training by the user is unlikely to be that useful for beginner EAL learners because mistakes may be replicated during the training process.

Supporting Writing

Using Writing Frames

There is a place for writing frames to be used with both beginner and more advanced EAL learners. However, they are unlikely to help new-to-English learners who need to concentrate first on developing their speaking and listening skills. Additionally, think carefully about their use with more able writers, as they can limit or confine the finished product.

Develop simple frames for beginner learners who find it hard to start or sustain writing beyond a couple of sentences. Distil the scope of the frame to a few key sentences, and provide starter words and phrases to help scaffold the writing. Imagine that you require an account of a class trip to the local zoo. An appropriate frame might look something like this.

> *To start with …*
> *Then …*
> *Next …*
> *After that …*
> *Finally …*

More advanced learners tend to write quite well, but they may have trouble with organizing their work or be reluctant to take risks with different types of phrases and connectives. Prepare more complex templates that offer the user a choice of words or phrases to scaffold their writing. Organize the frame into different sections to highlight how to organize the different elements of the text.

Writing text types such as discussion, explanation and persuasion can be particularly hard for some learners. Perhaps learners have been researching a topic and need to write a persuasive letter. A frame to support the bulk of the letter could be laid out in this way:

> Your view
> *I think that / My view is …*

Your reasons
The main reason is . . . because . . .
Also . . .
Moreover/additionally . . .
Finally . . .

Concluding the letter
To sum up / To conclude, I would like . . .
An acceptable solution/compromise would/
might/could be . . .

Most EAL learners will benefit from having access to their own topic mat throughout a unit of work. The most useful topic mats are A3 laminated charts containing specific language to assist with thinking and talking around a topic, as well as supporting academic writing.

It's important that this kind of resource looks 'professional'. Cluster similar types of language in boxes, and use plenty of little diagrams and symbols to reinforce meaning. It can help to leave a relatively sparse area in the centre of the mat where a learner can place a book or piece of paper yet still be able to see the main content.

The specific content on each chart will obviously vary according to subject area and the specific topic. Content might include small maps, timelines, graphs, diagrams and models. Language elements might be organized in any of the following ways:

- academic vocabulary;
- names of objects, places, characters or the like;
- descriptive words;
- comparative terms;
- frequently used connectives;
- words that explain patterns or trends in graphs.

There are plenty of free topic mats available on the internet, but you will probably want to download and adapt them to meet the specific needs of your learners.

Getting learners involved in producing their own graphic texts is a creative way of supporting writing across the curriculum. The graphical layout acts as a storyboard around which both formal description and informal speech-bubble dialogue can be constructed. It will help EAL learners if the texts can be directly linked to work they are currently undertaking within the mainstream curriculum.

For printed versions, photocopy the relevant sections and obscure the text within the narrative boxes and speech or thought bubbles. Alternatively, for digital versions take screen shots and edit out the relevant sections of text. The images can then be imported into a word processor, desktop publishing program or presentation package ready for learners to type in their own texts.

There are many useful software packages that allow you to create graphic texts from scratch. Some, like Kar2ouche, contain banks of curriculum-related materials – settings, characters, props, text boxes – that can be stitched together. Get learners to develop texts around historical events, geographical or scientific issues, biographies, instructional situations, traditional stories or personal narratives.

Other software – Comic Life, for example – is perfect for building graphic texts using real photographs. Using digital cameras, encourage groups to take freeze-frame photographs of themselves in appropriate settings and import them into the software alongside other digital images. Learners can choose from a range of graphic templates, add legends, speech or thought bubbles and develop narrative-based texts.

USEFUL RESOURCES
Kar2ouche – www.immersiveeducation.eu/index.php/
    kar2ouchepg
Comic Life – http://plasq.com/

Develop Graphic Texts

Explicit Grammar Teaching

Research into the writing of EAL learners (Ofsted 2003 & 2004) shows that less successful writers tend to fall down on specific grammatical elements, particularly the correct use of adverbials, modal verbs, prepositions, subject-verb agreement and verb tenses and endings.

Each school will need to consider the best approach to tackling these types of problems for advanced EAL writers. Bear in mind that learners acquire language most successfully in the context of the curriculum rather than through decontextualized drills or vocabulary exercises. This is particularly important for withdrawal intervention sessions that focus on specific aspects of grammar.

The 2007 Excellence and Enjoyment materials contain a programme for guided teaching sessions that can be used to address specific aspects of grammar for advanced EAL learners. The materials come with a useful set of Clicker (Idea 77 on p. 112) grids that can be used to support text-construction exercises using pictures and speech.

Language Garden has been successfully used with EAL learners to help them develop a greater variety of sentence structures during creative writing. Using the metaphor of a growing plant, colourful branching stories can be built up in stages, modelling the differing purposes for verbs, adjectives, prepositions and so on. There are two resources, one with 60 ready-made materials centred on specific topics and focusing on different aspects of grammar. Each unit is built around an initial story; learning is thus rooted within a clear context. A range of activities, including gap fills, dictionary tasks and the identification of parts of speech, is offered. The second, newly released resource lets learners make their own language gardens so that all learners can be creative.

USEFUL RESOURCES

DfES (2002). 'Grammar for Writing: Supporting pupils learning EAL' – http://www.naldic.org.uk/Teaching-and-Learning/ealgrammar.pdf

DfES (2007). 'Excellence and Enjoyment: Learning and teaching for bilingual children in the primary years' – http://media.education.gov.uk/assets/files/pdf/e/ excellence and enjoyment learning and teaching for bilingual children in the primary years.pdf

Language Garden – www.languagegarden.com/

Cameron, L. (2003). 'Writing in English as an Additional Language at Key Stage 4 and post-16'. London: OfSTED.

Cameron, L. (2004). 'Writing in English as an Additional Language at Key Stage 4 and post-16'. London: OfSTED.

Wordle

Wordle is a free online tool that enables a user to produce word clouds based on the frequency of words in a digital text (including words in different languages). It has many applications for teachers working with EAL learners, particularly those who are at more advanced stages of learning English.

The ability to visually produce word clouds, where the size of each word indicates how frequently it appears in a text, is particularly supportive of language learning because it can focus attention on:

- subject-specific vocabulary;
- the interconnectedness of related words;
- process words and connectives that predominate in different literary genres.

Here are some ideas for how teachers and learners can use Wordle both in the classroom and during out-of-hours learning:

- At the beginning of a new piece of work, try producing a word cloud from a topic summary or essay that covers the salient points; learners can pick out some of the key vocabulary and check the meaning if needed.
- Topic Wordles can also be used as quick revision guides.
- Opinion-based texts can be analysed using Wordle in order to support learners' understanding of the particular position taken by the author.
- Two or more Wordles can be compared in order to demonstrate how word usage changes according to era, genre, text type and so on.
- Personal writing can be analysed in order to support redrafting – for example, showing how lower level writing might have an overabundance of certain verbs, adjectives or common connectives, such as 'and'. (You will need to change the settings in Wordle to allow what it labels 'common words' to be displayed, as the default setting automatically removes these words from the final output.)

As Wordle allows a user to alter many visual attributes of the word cloud, it provides an opportunity for learning more about media literacy and presentational impact. Finished Wordles also provide ready-made assessment opportunities for practitioners since they can be printed or saved for future viewing.

USEFUL RESOURCES
Wordle – www.wordle.net/
Wordsift – www.wordsift.com/

As EAL learners become more proficient in their use of language across the curriculum, they learn to build 'chunks' of language from vocabulary in their immediate lexicon. However, learning which words go naturally together and which do not can be very challenging. For example, it is more natural in English to say 'increase speed' rather than 'raise speed', although the use of the word 'raise' in this context is quite logical.

Collocation describes the tendency for certain words to occur next to each other in speech and writing. There are many ways to help older, more advanced EAL learners grasp colloquial collocations, as well as more academic ones from different subject areas:

● Ensure any work on collocations has a clear context, such as reading and writing familiar stories or non-fiction tasks within subject areas.
● Point out groups of colloquial collocations that are idiomatic in nature: 'give and take', 'give and go', 'give the game away', 'give notice' and so on.
● Get learners to build up academic collocation lists; in history, for example, phrases such as 'take/make a decision' or 'make/give/express/offer an opinion'.
● Develop curriculum-related activities, including text-marking incorrect collocations or matching collocations with meanings.
● Encourage the use of advanced internet search tools; searching for 'increase speed', for example, returns many more hits than 'raise speed', showing that the former phrase is much more widely used. (Note that it's vital to enclose the two words in inverted commas.)
● Install and use concordance software, which is useful for showing collocation and analysing texts relating to different subjects.
● Experiment with online visual dictionaries (e.g., Visual Thesaurus); here, looking up 'move', returns a number of links, including 'move on', 'move up', 'move out', move over'.

USEFUL RESOURCES
Visual Thesaurus – www.visualthesaurus.com/
Visuwords – www.visuwords.com/

Modern word processors contain a number of inbuilt supports for writing. However, for certain EAL learners some tools will be more appropriate than others. Used inappropriately, certain tools used by emergent writers can be more confusing than helpful, while more advanced learners may come to rely on tools that they don't actually need. Correct use of each tool needs to be specifically taught.

Since learners who are new to English often worry about the number of errors they make, as indicated by the spelling- and grammar-checking feature, real-time error checking can be turned off. (More confident beginners, on the other hand, might appreciate having access to real-time spelling and grammar checking, as this will help them identify their mistakes and give them the option to make corrections.) However, the 'auto-correct' feature will be helpful because it seamlessly corrects a whole raft of basic errors. Being free from the worry of making simple errors can help less confident writers focus on the more immediate task of constructing cohesive texts. The thesaurus will probably be unhelpful, as it may refer learners to too many unfamiliar or new words. (The thesaurus will be more useful to advanced learners, who will have a wider vocabulary and thus be able to make more informed choices.) Text-to-speech technology can help with self-correction because it can be interfaced with word processors to help learners hear what they have written. As long as learners understand what they are doing, the 'find and replace' feature can also save a lot of time.

All the aforementioned tools can be useful for more advanced learners, but be aware that overreliance can mask systematic errors or hide more serious problems.

Learners who are literate in L1 may benefit from having online access so that they can use real-time translation to help them transfer knowledge across languages.

Clicker has been used extensively with EAL learners, particularly beginners, to help them develop writing skills in English and other languages. The application provides a range of media-based tools, including a comprehensive bank of picture vocabulary, audio playback of writing through text-to-speech synthesis and the ability for learners to record their own voice. Automatic error-checking facilities assist with spelling and punctuation. Modules of curriculum-support materials organized into topics can be purchased alongside free resources built into 'learning grids'.

Effective use of Clicker requires planning:

- ensure that learners understand how to use the application interface;
- focus on specific aspects of writing, such as connectives, powerful verbs and topic vocabulary;
- encourage learners to record their voice and compare it to pre-recorded models;
- allow learners to write in L1 where appropriate;
- try to develop creative writing within the context of pre-built Clicker talking books;
- purchase and use the pre-built topic materials for non-fiction writing;
- download free topic/literacy materials from the Learning Grids website.

USEFUL RESOURCES
Learning Grids – www.learninggrids.com/
Clicker – www.cricksoft.com/uk/products/tools/clicker/ home.aspx
A set of new-to-English materials has also been developed –www.cricksoft.com/uk/products/content/ nte/default.aspx

WriteOnline is a software program that offers a range of supports for developing writing. It is most suitable for use with older, more advanced EAL learners because it has a sophisticated interface, featuring powerful tools that require an understanding of vocabulary and grammar beyond that of most new-to-English learners. The software is highly configurable; the level of support can be matched to each learner's needs.

To illustrate how WriteOnline can be used, consider Hakim, a year-8 EAL learner who has been studying English for about two years and has been asked to write a few paragraphs about different types of energy in a science class.

As Hakim begins to write, he has access to a layout of menus and tools familiar from word processors he has used before. Once he has written his first sentence, the inbuilt text-to-speech synthesis automatically plays back his writing, providing him with an authentic oral model and assisting him with error checking. As he has problems with spelling, the red underlining focuses his attention on incorrectly spelled words. By right-clicking he can access lists of alternative words that are also audio-enabled.

Hakim notices that to the right of the page, words begin to appear in a list as he types. This word prediction allows him to quickly select the word he needs from a list and paste it into his writing. Moreover, because he still sometimes attempts phonetic spelling, 'physical' appears in the list as he types 'fizical'. Word prediction also presents words contextually, rather like a writing frame. As he thinks how to start his next sentence, he is presented with words that naturally appear at a sentence's beginning, and when he needs a specific grammatical construct, a list of appropriate words becomes available.

Hakim also uses an 'energy' topic word bar that has been created by his teacher. The word bar presents a set of alphabetically ordered key words and phrases at the bottom of the screen. This bar reminds him to use more academic language in his science writing.

USEFUL RESOURCE

Write Online – www.cricksoft.com/uk/products/tools/ writeonline/

Promoting an Intercultural Dimension

Dual-Language Storytelling

Running a dual-language storytelling session is a perfect way to involve bilingual adults and children from the whole school community. Try auditing the bilingual skills of practitioners, learners and parents, in order to identify suitable volunteers to participate in a storytelling session. You may be able to source bilingual adults from key workers in the local authority, and it is also possible to hold a story session over a videoconferencing link (Idea 91 on p. 133).

Choose stories that build upon the languages and traditions of the major communities attending the school. Hearing different languages used within formal situations will raise the status of EAL learners and enrich the lives of all learners.

Suitable opportunities for a bilingual storytelling session might involve the following events:

- welcoming a new learner to the school;
- preparing for a digital storytelling project (Ideas 46–47 on pp. 64–66);
- celebrating a religious festival;
- supporting a cultural event like Gypsy Roma Traveller Month;
- promoting an international event such as European Day of Languages.

Collect a range of resources to support the storytelling session, such as dressing-up clothes, props, musical instruments and puppets. Suitable music can enrich the experience for the audience, and it may be possible to project images from the book onto an interactive whiteboard (IWB) or, alternatively, set the storytelling to a piece of drama created by the learners. It is generally good practice to read or retell the first section of the story in the other language and then alternate with English throughout.

Looking at mathematics from a geographical and historical perspective can greatly contribute to the development of an intercultural dimension within the curriculum while supporting EAL learners in their work. It can also provide an opportunity for EAL learners to demonstrate knowledge and skill in mathematics from their own linguistic or cultural background that might otherwise be ignored.

Here are some ideas for activities:

- Investigate the contributions of people from across the world to the development of mathematics; for example, early Muslim Arabic scholars and Indian mathematicians.
- Learn about some famous 'discoveries' – for example, the use of zero as a placeholder and the golden ratio.
- Find out about the lives of influential mathematicians from across the world.
- Look at some of the interesting connections between mathematics and other subjects such as art, music and architecture.
- Discover where mathematical words have come from; for example, 'algebra', 'circle' and 'centre'.
- Investigate the importance of specific numbers to some cultures; for example, lucky and unlucky numbers.
- Make and/or play some maths games from around the world; for example, Alquerque, Shisima and Mancala.
- Utilize realia from around the world for number work; for example, menus, product labels or money.
- Practise counting to 10 in different languages.
- Learn how to write numerals and numbers in different number systems, ancient and modern.
- Find out about different base systems – binary (2), Mayan (20), Babylonian (60) and others.
- Try doing simple calculations using different number systems.

Cross-Cultural Mathematics

- Research counting and calculating equipment from around the world; for example, abacus, quipu, Napier's rods.
- Identify different ways of solving mathematical problems; for example, Egyptian multiplication and the gelosia and grid methods.

Many schools choose to celebrate the pluri-lingual nature of their community by focusing on a different language each month during the academic year. This is an excellent way of drawing upon the language skills of the EAL population and boosting their self-esteem. Of course, this type of enrichment activity is beneficial for any school wanting to develop an intercultural dimension within the curriculum.

Here are some suggested activities:

- Have learners answer the register in the target language.
- Create a display featuring the chosen language; where possible, tie in countries and cultures.
- Host an assembly about the language of the month.
- Conduct language taster sessions; where possible, this should involve EAL learners and their parents.
- Prepare a library box with relevant resources: bilingual books, dual-language dictionaries and so on.
- Record audio and video exemplars of learners using the language, and host the results on the school's VLE.
- Dovetail activities with national or international events; for example, European Languages Day, the Olympics or the World Cup.

USEFUL RESOURCES

Newbury Park: Language of the month – www. newburypark.redbridge.sch.uk/langofmonth/

Portsmouth: Language of the half-term – www.school-portal.co.uk/GroupWorkspaces.asp?GroupId=922202 &WorkspaceId=1974203

European Day of Languages – http://edl.ecml.at/

Language of the Month

Throughout the year there are numerous religious, social and political events that can be woven into the curriculum. It's a good idea to tie these events into the curriculum at the beginning of the academic year.

Sign up for the Shap calendar, which details all the major religious festivals and celebrations, and keep a note of other national and international days.

Apart from religious festivals, some events provide natural opportunities to tackle difficult and complex issues. For example, in January, Holocaust Memorial Day offers the chance to study aspects of prejudice and genocide in history, RE or citizenship. Every June there is the potential to discuss issues of migration and asylum through Gypsy Roma Traveller History Month and Refugee Week. October brings Black History Month, and 'Show Racism the Red Card' always has a fortnight of action during this month.

USEFUL RESOURCES

Shap Calendar – www.shapworkingparty.org.uk/calendar.
   html

Show Racism the Red Card – www.srtrc.org/

Capitalize on the Yearly Events Calendar

Infusing the whole curriculum with a truly intercultural dimension doesn't happen overnight. It can't be treated as a 'tick-box' exercise, where 'visiting' other countries or cultures only happens on special occasions. A whole-school focus requires the full commitment of all the staff and learners at the school, as well as that of the wider community.

Here are some simple suggestions:

- Don't just organize one-off events that touch upon culture and language; this can be seen as rather tokenistic.
- Plan topics or themes at specific times of the year to naturally coincide with festivals, international days and the like, in order to seamlessly integrate them into the curriculum.
- Actively seek out opportunities for intercultural work right across the curriculum; for example, cross-cultural mathematics and language (Idea 80 on p. 117);
- Offer a balanced view when considering life in other countries, particularly those in the 'developing world'; for example, show images of high-tech city living alongside quieter, simpler village life.
- Think about use of language, and try to avoid references like 'they' or 'them' or 'this is how *we* do such-and-such'.
- Check that books and digital resources are routinely scrutinized for stereotype and bias.
- Ensure that relevant resource material is on display and in classrooms throughout the year, rather than being wheeled out just for special days.
- Where possible, draw upon the linguistic and cultural knowledge of the experts, EAL learners and their parents or carers, for assemblies and celebration events, as well to directly support class-based learning.

How to Avoid Stereotype and Tokenism within the Curriculum

Taking the time to learn about social and cultural norms specific to certain communities can help avoid potentially embarrassing situations. Simple adjustments to the way we interact with people and correctly interpreting body language and similar behaviours will greatly improve effectiveness in dealing with learners and their parents or carers.

First, ideas about personal space can vary across cultures:

- In some traditions people stand much closer when they are communicating.
- Sometimes individuals don't like to be touched by people outside the family circle; for example, the head in some cultures is considered sacred.
- Some Muslim girls and women will not shake hands with members of the opposite gender.

Body language and interactions can sometimes be misleading:

- Learners may avoid eye contact with adults who are speaking to them, since in some cultures this is a sign of respect.
- Some learners will nod and smile often during conversation, but this does not imply that they have fully understood.
- Also, conventions for showing understanding or agreement can vary, so much so that sometimes a nod of the head can mean 'no' and a shake 'yes'.
- Languages that rely heavily on tone to convey meaning can sound harsh to an untrained ear; thus, ordinary conversation in L1 might sound rather abrupt or aggressive. Also, certain forms or conventions can make language seem more direct; for example, use of 'will', as opposed to 'should' or 'could', can make the user sound rather bossy. Nuances like this often unintentionally transfer over when a bilingual person uses English.

Persona Dolls are realistic dolls that can be transformed into 'little people' by providing them with their own personalities. Skilled practitioners can identify opportune moments to 'invite' them into classrooms to facilitate non-threatening discussion around sensitive and thought-provoking issues. Young children quickly identify with the dolls to the extent of seeing them as small friends. As the children begin to empathize, they may feel happy, sad or excited; they may offer helpful suggestions and words of support for the worries and problems that the doll may present.

Practitioners should attend Persona doll training in order to ensure the most effective results.

RUNNING A SESSION

1. How to build the doll's persona
   The 'persona' should be introduced during the session as naturally as possible. How much or little of this is revealed will vary, depending on the purpose of the session, the age of the participating children and whether or not the doll is to become a regular visitor to the classroom. Interaction with the doll should be like holding a real child, including pretending to listen to the doll's comments and recasting them to the children.

2. Develop an appropriate scenario; for example:
   - explore different lifestyles and types of family structures: such as being from a Traveller background;
   - share life experiences: living abroad and moving from another country;
   - celebrate diversity: knowing other languages or having a different faith;
   - introduce special events: festivals and remembrance days;

Using Persona Dolls

- address sensitive issues: trauma, disability, discrimination and racism.
3. To prepare, you need to:
    - invent a realistic background; for example, name, family structure, country of origin, ethnicity, knowledge of languages, religion;
    - source relevant photographs: family members, pets, home, famous places, places of worship;
    - collect appropriate artefacts or media: favourite toys, clothing, food, religious artefacts, maps, music;
    - bind the materials together in a suitable format; for example, a suitcase, a photograph album or diary or scrapbook.
4. Questioning and promoting discussion

It is a good idea to have prepared a number of specific 'questions' to promote participation from the audience while maintaining flexibility when responding to their contributions.

USEFUL RESOURCE
www.persona-doll-training.org/ukhome.html

Home-School Links

How Schools Work Video

New-arrival families will really appreciate information about their child's new school in as accessible a format as possible. For that matter, so may families who have been here for a generation. Try involving the whole school community in the production of a video to explain all the essential information. Where possible, get learners involved in planning, filming, editing and writing or recording the narration. Ask bilingual learners, parents and practitioners to help with producing high-quality translations, and dub the video in those languages most significant to the school's context.

The specific contents of such a video will vary from school to school, and it can sometimes be difficult to predict which elements will or will not be helpful. Try interviewing a range of BME children and adults to elicit what information would have been most useful in preparation for starting school. There will be common elements whether the learner is British born or newly arrived from abroad.

It may help to split the final video into different sections, so that families can access the bits that seem most relevant to them; any information that you deem essential can be marked as such. Once it is finished, you can place the video onto DVD or place it onto the school's VLE.

Organizing family learning events is an effective way to encourage greater participation from parents or carers in their children's education. Invite the whole family to attend sessions where everyone learns together. Depending on your focus, you will need to decide on which combination of parents to invite to any specific session. There may be a particular issue with parents or carers from a specific ethnic background, or perhaps you may want to target families of new-arrival learners. Many schools use family learning to promote community cohesion by inviting families from different ethnic backgrounds alongside white British families.

How you organize family learning is another important consideration. A sequence of sessions around a particular theme is likely to have greater impact than a one-off event. Timing is also critical, as you will need to decide the length of each session and the time of day that is likely to attract the most families. Consider laying on transport or ensuring that invited parents or carers have the option of a lift from someone else attending. Don't give up if turnout is low on the first attempt. Word will get round, and participation tends to improve the more sessions you arrange.

For parents or carers, family learning events can be used to:

- find out about how schools work;
- learn how to cook a dish from another country;
- get some ideas on how to support their child with homework;
- experience what school examinations are like;
- identify the best ways to read with their child;
- learn about safe use of the internet.

Early Language Development

Talk with parents or carers as soon as an EAL child starts school, and reinforce the school's position on early language development and the importance of maintaining L1. This will be important not only for the reception child but also for younger siblings.

First, ensure parents or carers understand that research unequivocally supports the benefits of a multilingual upbringing. Natural exposure to more than one spoken language as a child grows up is very common across the world. Should the child go on to develop literacy in more than one language, then hearing and learning to talk in those languages is obviously beneficial. This is as important for British-born children as for those who are new arrivals. When neither parent or carer speaks English well, it is best to sensitively suggest that initially they only use L1 at home. This can be reviewed at a later date, and at some later point siblings may choose to converse in English rather than L1.

Some families have lost the art of using songs and rhymes to engage their children. You may find it useful to initiate a family learning session to introduce parents or carers to traditional British songs and nursery rhymes, and it may be useful to elicit ones from their own cultural background. Try recording songs or rhymes from Britain and other countries onto a CD and loan it out to families with young children.

Explain the importance of exposing children to bilingual print from an early age. Direct parents or carers to local sources such as road and shop signs, menus, food labels and newspapers. Encourage them to read to their children from bilingual texts, and get them to make reference to both language scripts so that their children become familiar with the written form of the languages that they are hearing or learning as they grow up.

USEFUL RESOURCES

Talk to Your Baby (in different languages) – www.literacytrust.org.uk/talk_to_your_baby/resources/418_q
Developing Reading Skills Through Home Language – http://emat.redbridge.lgfl.digitalbrain.com/lgfl/leas/redbridge/schools/emat/web/EAL/DevRdgSkillsOrder/

There are many reasons why EAL learners make extended visits to their country of origin. This needs to be seen as a learning opportunity.

Here are some ideas for supporting learners when they make extended visits abroad:

- Ensure that learners have access to the school's VLE, and where possible, develop activities that enable them to continue studies when abroad.
- Provide learners with a disposable camera so they can take pictures on their trip abroad.
- Where possible, entrust learners with digital media equipment to take pictures or record sounds.
- Encourage learners to keep a diary of their exploits on their visit.
- Suggest that learners collect interesting resources to show classmates on their return: food labels, menus, newspapers, toys, musical instruments, games and the like.

When learners return, they could share their experience:

- by performing a show-and-tell for their classmates about some aspect of their trip;
- by contributing to an assembly about their country or cultural background;
- by making a talking book (Idea 48 on p. 67) about their trip abroad.

USEFUL RESOURCE

Extended Visits Workbook: Bangladesh and Pakistan
KS2 – Oldham EMSS, Sandwell EMAP, Sheffield EMAS

Activities for Learners Who Take Extended Visits Abroad

Reaching Out to the Wider Community

Videoconferencing (Vc)

Most schools nowadays have the capability to use basic videoconferencing technology. Not only is the equipment (web camera and microphone) very affordable, but there are free solutions such as Skype™ and Flashmeeting. Many local authorities also promote their own solutions, such as Macromedia Breeze™.

Videoconferencing is an essential tool for communication at a distance, locally, nationally and even internationally. Since it enables speakers of other languages to practise their oral skills, it is perfect for learning languages in general. EAL learners can also develop questioning and interview skills in the target language – that is, English. When learners from similar and different backgrounds can socialize together or work on curriculum-related projects within any subject area, community cohesion is enhanced. Experts from BME communities can be 'invited' into the classroom to share skills and experiences and act as positive role models. Practitioners can also use VC to liaise together and develop their expertise in managing ethnic-minority achievement.

Planning for a VC session:

- book a quiet room or area for the session;
- ensure that all the equipment is working;
- check that the VC client works; some local authorities block certain software – for example, Skype™ is often blocked, although Flashmeeting tends to work everywhere;
- ensure that when learners are communicating together, they are always supervised by an adult;
- note that some VC software allows users to record the session for playback at a later date; while this can be very useful, it is important to check parental permissions when children and young people are involved.

1. Linking isolated EAL learners

Many schools have relatively small numbers of BME learners, and often their EAL population tends to be culturally and linguistically isolated; this can also be true of their families. It is a good idea to identify same-language speakers in other isolated situations in order to facilitate communication through a VC link. This allows EAL learners the opportunity to practise L1 and socialize with those of a similar age and background.

2. Community Cohesion – linking learners from mainly white schools with those from ethnically diverse settings (and vice versa)

This is a useful way of enabling white British learners to meet and interact with learners with whom they would not normally have contact because of the locality of their school or home. In this way individuals and groups can socialize together or take part in more structured activities that look at the commonality and differences between people. It can be a useful way to prepare for learner-exchange visits and can also facilitate follow-up work.

3. 'Ask the Experts' from BME communities

Invite members of local community groups to become experts for the day. Using VC technology, the 'experts' can enter classrooms virtually to talk about lifestyle or to showcase their own expertise in work, religious practice or a creative talent. Try linking this with special celebrations or national or international events [Idea 82 on page xx.]. Learners can develop their interview technique and learn about experiences beyond their immediate context.

4. Bilingual Q&A sessions for parents of new arrivals

Organizing events where a bilingual practitioner is at the end of a VC link at a pre-arranged time can be useful to enable parents to ask questions in L1 about education and other related matters. This will help not only their

IDEA

91

Five Ideas for Using Videoconferencing (Vc)

school-aged children but also older siblings in terms of signposting them on to further education.

5. Bilingual storytelling

One practitioner can efficiently deliver a bilingual storytelling session to lots of learners in different schools. This will help raise the self-esteem of EAL learners who know the same language because they can become experts for the day. Besides supporting language learning and contributing to the intercultural dimension of the curriculum, it will also be enriching for monolingual learners.

USEFUL RESOURCES

Using VC to support community cohesion: South East Grid for Learning (SEGfL) – http://microsites2.segfl. org.uk/2coco

Sometimes schools do not know how to make the best use of the resource base that is available through the various ethnic, cultural and religious groups within the local community. Consider making this a core responsibility for a member of staff.

Most of the major BME groups in the area will have an official association that represents them. If you are seeking information about the history and culture of a specific group, then this is a good starting point.

Find out which employers in the area have recruited from abroad; audit the area for shops, businesses, and religious centres to get some useful contacts. Inviting successful role models from BME communities to the school is a way of enriching the curriculum and helps with identifying potential speakers for assemblies. You may be able to identify suitable places for school visits in order to support the teaching of certain subjects like RE and business studies. Having such contacts may also be useful for finding suitable work experience placements.

Knowing what services are on offer in the local authority will really benefit newly arrived families. This is particularly true for learners from refugee or asylum-seeking families, as you will be able to recommend to them specific points of contact, such as legal services and charitable groups in the area.

New-arrival families will really appreciate knowing where and when local community language classes can be found, as well as which colleges offer ESOL classes. You will need to work with local colleges to develop clear guidelines for which type of learners to enrol in English-language courses. Certain late arrivals in KS4 may benefit from part-time attendance at college, or you may want to bring in external tutors to run classes in school for a targeted group of learners.

Accessing Resources within the Local Community

Many learners have linguistic, cultural and religious lives that rarely interface with school life unless a robust effort is made to encourage this sort of interaction.

Find out whether EAL learners are continuing to study L1 outside of school. For some this may be an informal home-based approach, while for others it will be at Saturday or Sunday community-language classes. Many EAL learners take language exams each year, and their achievements should be recognized by the school.

Celebrate the fact that some learners have deeply religious lives that put major time constraints on their home life; dealing with this situation usually requires significant discipline. They may study a holy book, regularly attend a place of worship or have experienced a rite of passage at a particular age. Older Muslim children may fast during Ramadan; this can be another opportunity to credit learners for their achievements.

Ask learners what responsibilities they have at home; for example, interpreting and translating information for parents, caring for younger siblings and elderly relatives, working within a family business. Where these responsibilities are proportionate to the age of the learner, schools may want to consider developing flexible arrangements that support each learner's individual home circumstances.

It is vital to keep accurate records of this kind of information and ensure that all relevant staff are kept informed. Passing on these records at the point of transition will be hugely beneficial for the learners themselves as well as for the receiving school.

There can be many benefits from linking with schools locally, nationally or even internationally. Having educational links with a diverse range of schools provides opportunities to support community cohesion and develop a culturally infused curriculum.

How and when you decide to initiate linking projects will depend on the specific character of your school. Generally contact starts through a series of email exchanges, although communication can be enhanced through simple videoconferencing [Ideas 90–91 on pp. 132–3]. You may decide to run projects in out-of-hours settings in order that learners can communicate in a fairly informal way.

Alternatively, projects can be tied more directly into the curriculum through English, humanities and the creative arts. Try developing projects that require learners to compare and contrast locality, history or lifestyle. There is opportunity here to exchange art works or musical compositions or to initiate joint writing projects. Make a point of creating activities that challenge learners' perceptions of the world around them. Also, encourage learners to communicate through different languages; this enables EAL learners to practise L1 and supports the overall delivery of languages across the school.

Successful school-linking projects frequently lead to learner exchanges and all the learning opportunities that this entails. Exchanges can be significant moments in a learner's life: the first time visiting a city, the countryside or the coast; the first time to really socialize with someone of a different ethnicity or religious persuasion; the first visit to another country.

USEFUL RESOURCES
British Council World Links and Partnerships www. britishcouncil.org/schoolpartnerships.htm

School-Linking Projects

Whole School Approaches

All schools will benefit from a senior manager who leads on ethnic minority achievement (EMA), although experience shows it is an area of provision that necessarily involves the whole school community. Many schools, particularly those with significant numbers of BME learners, build a team of practitioners to work with new arrivals, help deliver intervention sessions and support classroom practitioners in developing sound EAL practice.

Here are some specific tasks for anyone who has recently inherited this role or is looking to develop it further:

- Clearly identify roles and responsibilities within the school so that the key tasks do not fall upon the shoulders of just one person.
- Develop a specific policy for 'race equality' and ensure that references to EMA are made within other relevant ones: inclusion, assessment, anti-bullying and so on.
- Audit the school population and ensure that the data captures ethnicity, date of birth, date of arrival in the United Kingdom, L1, religion, country of origin and other essential information.
- Develop tracking systems to monitor both attainment and progress of BME learners; you need to be able to make comparisons between different ethnic groups and the white British (WBRI) population, as well as identify the rate of progress for any individual learner.
- Establish an ongoing programme of continuing professional development (CPD) for all the staff in school; areas for training should include a focus on strategies to support beginner and advanced learners and on how to promote cultural diversity through the curriculum and race-equality training (including how to report and record racist incidents).

USEFUL RESOURCES

DCSF (2009). 'Ensuring the attainment of more advanced learners of English as an additional language (EAL)'.

DCSF (2007). 'New Arrivals Excellence Programme: Guidance (Primary)'.

DfES (2006). 'Excellence and Enjoyment: Learning and teaching for bilingual children in the primary years'.

Conducting a Learning Environment Walk

How welcoming does the school feel to families, children and young people from BME backgrounds? This is an important question, because the learning environment inevitably communicates something about the school's attitude towards inclusion in its widest sense.

Experience suggests that a learning-environment audit is best performed by two or more practitioners – perhaps a senior manager involved with ethnic-minority achievement and a governor with responsibility for inclusion. It is also an activity which could involve BME parents and the school council.

The school office is often the first point of contact for many families and a good place to start the 'walk'. What is your immediate impression as you enter this area? Are there dual-language welcome signs and positive images that reflect the full diversity of the school population? Could the phone system present a barrier to communication? Even when the school has a low percentage of BME/EAL learners, these are still important considerations.

What about the corridors, classrooms and other school areas? Look out for these elements:

- intercultural displays that demonstrate the school's commitment to developing a culturally infused curriculum;
- dual-language material that celebrates the many languages used within the school community;
- examples of work from BME learners, including beginner EAL learners;
- photographs of people drawn from a range of ethnic backgrounds, including successful role models from the world of work;
- teaching and learning resources that promote differentiation; for example, dual-language, multimedia displays;
- classroom organization that shows evidence of flexibility in grouping arrangements for all learners.

Does the library or IRC stock a good range of dual-language dictionaries, bilingual books and stories from other cultures? Are books and audio-visual materials routinely checked to avoid stereotype and/or tokenism?

While conducting this kind of audit, it's also worth taking a virtual tour of the school's online presence, including the public-facing website and the internal look and feel of the school's virtual learning environment (VLE).

Running a Young-Interpreter Scheme

Young-interpreter schemes capitalize on the huge potential within each school to use the linguistic and social skills of all their learners to support the development of an inclusive and welcoming environment for EAL learners and their families.

Training forms an essential part of the scheme. Bilingual learners learn how to utilize their L1 skills to assist with interpreting and translation when working with beginner EAL learners, particularly new arrivals and their families. English-only speakers also work alongside bilingual learners to employ strategies and resources for giving support in situations where an L1 is not shared between learners and adults.

A young-interpreter scheme goes way beyond arranging peer buddies (Idea 7 on p. 14) for new-arrival EAL learners. Potential activities permeate the whole school, from promoting cultural and linguistic diversity to working with families and supporting individual EAL learners in and out of the classroom.

Potential activities can include the following:

- showing visitors and new-arrival families around the school;
- inducting and settling new learners;
- using interpreting skills to facilitate home-school communication;
- where appropriate, translating written material;
- supporting peers in the classroom;
- offering taster language sessions for peers and school staff.

USEFUL RESOURCE

Hampshire Young Interpreter Scheme – www3.hants.gov. uk/education/ema/ema-schools/ema-good-practice/ ema-pupil-interpreters/ema-hyis.htm

If you are looking for a way to initiate a whole-school focus on speaking and listening, then you might want to consider implementing 'Talking Partners', a highly successful programme that was initially developed for EAL learners but has since been used effectively with other learners.

'Talking Partners' is a short-term intervention aimed at boosting oral skills for targeted learners in order to produce confident and independent learners. Led by a trained practitioner, the sessions are based around practical, collaborative games and activities where speaking and listening are central to learning. Effective modelling by the lead practitioner is key to the success of the programme. Planning between the facilitator and class teacher ensures that the content of each session is linked directly to the mainstream curriculum.

The programme is run over ten weeks, where one practitioner works with three learners for three sessions per week. Each session is completely oral, starting with a five-minute warm-up followed by a specific focus – for example, talking about a specific story or text, analysing the text in more detail and developing or telling new stories. Throughout each session the facilitator keeps detailed notes about each child's progress on a range of indicators.

'Talking Maths' is organized in a very similar way. Rather than teaching mathematics discretely, there is a heavy emphasis on speaking and listening using games and activities to focus on the understanding and use of mathematical language. Implementing 'Talking Maths' enables learners to be more precise in their use of language to explain and justify their mathematical thinking and has been shown to raise their participation levels in mainstream classes.

Any school wishing to implement either of these programmes should send one or more lead practitioners to a training event, where they will also receive a comprehensive set of support materials. A key manager should also oversee the running of these programmes.

Talking Partners and Talking Maths

Over time, schools will benefit from cascading training down to other staff and incorporating the approaches back into the mainstream curriculum, thereby developing a whole-school emphasis on speaking and listening.

USEFUL RESOURCES

Talking Partners: Education Bradford

Talking Maths: Liverpool City Council, EMTAS – http://liverpool.gov.uk/schools-and-learning/support-for-ethnic-minorities/

Online professional networks offer practitioners a really practical way to develop EAL practice and pedagogy. Joining any one of these user groups will bring you into contact with professionals working on a range of bilingual and race-equality issues. If you have a pressing question, you can be sure that someone on the list will know the answer or be able to point you in the right direction to find what you need.

User groups work on the basis of email lists, where a user can see the contributions made by anyone else in the group. All email conversations are open and can be tracked by following the 'thread' of each conversation. Additionally, past conversations can be searched for and reviewed.

To join a professional network, do the following:

1. point your web browser at the home page of the group (see links below);
2. make sure you have a valid Yahoo or Google email in order to be able to subscribe to any one of their user groups;
3. join the group by filling in your details and choosing login names and passwords;
4. Customize your profile as you want, including by
   – electing to have emails sent to any other valid email address;
   – choosing whether to receive individual emails or a daily digest.

USEFUL RESOURCES

EAL-Bilingual (all things connected with EAL and bilingual teaching and learning) – http://groups.google.com/group/eal-bilingual

Refed (a group for practitioners working with learners from refugee and asylum seeking backgrounds) – http://groups.yahoo.com/group/refed

COCONetwork (useful for practitioners wanting to develop expertise in community cohesion). http://groups.yahoo.com/group/coconetwork

You may also like to join a Twitter group where you can exchange quick ideas with like-minded colleagues.

NALDIC – http://twitter.com/#!/naldic

ESL Twibe – www.twibes.com/group/ESL

One of the most comprehensive websites around belongs to the National Association for Language Development in the Curriculum (NALDIC). This site offers a good balance between theoretical research and practical teaching and learning pedagogy. There are numerous downloadable articles, documents and media clips – www.naldic.org.uk/.

It's worth doing a search for relevant local-authority websites around the United Kingdom. An internet search for keywords like 'ethnic minority achievement service' will find the most useful ones. There are many notable sites, but 'Emas4Success' is particularly good – www.emas4success.org/.

Another excellent site is 'Ethnic Minority Achievement Online', a collaboration of Birmingham, Leeds and Manchester LAs. It is a one-stop jumping-off point for resources to support this area of work – www.emaonline.org.uk/ema/.

If you want to find out how to develop intercultural approaches within the curriculum, then you will find Leicestershire's 'iRespect' website particularly useful. The site offers advice and guidance around issues connected with race equality and cultural diversity, including downloadable teaching ideas, materials and lesson plans – www.irespect.net/.

Many other sites offer downloadable teaching materials; one of the best is the Collaborative Learning Project, which hosts activities created *by* teachers *for* teachers. Developed over many years, the site is a cornucopia of downloadable activities aimed at developing the oral skills of EAL learners – www.collaborativelearning.org/.

For older EAL learners, there are numerous learn-English sites that host appropriate materials. Keyword searches for 'ESL' and 'ESOL' will reveal sites containing podcasts, videos, lesson plans and flash-based games for the teaching of English. A good place to start is the British Council's 'Teaching English' site – www.teachingenglish.org.uk/.

Six of the Best from the Internet